How to Be a Star Associate

A Guide to Excelling in Your Early Legal Career

JAMES J. MCDONALD, JR.

AMERICAN BAR ASSOCIATION

Tort Trial and Insurance Practice Section

Cover design by Carolina Martinez/ABA Design

Printed in the United States of America.

28 27 26 25 24   5 4 3 2 1

A catalog record for this book is available from the Library of Congress.

Discounts are available for books ordered in bulk. Special consideration is given to state bars, CLE programs, and other bar-related organizations. Inquire at Book Publishing, ABA Publishing, American Bar Association, 321 N. Clark Street, Chicago, Illinois 60654-7598.

www.shopABA.org

Contents

3

Doing the Work 43

4

Your Written Work Product 71

About the Author

James J. McDonald, Jr. has practiced labor and employment law with Fisher & Phillips LLP for more than 40 years. It all started with a dinner party with a harpist that brought him, as a summer associate, to the firm in Atlanta (see Chapter 1). After six years in Atlanta, he set out to build a practice for the firm in Southern California, and for 24 years he managed what became the firm's largest office, in Irvine, California. He currently practices in the firm's Irvine and Tampa offices, and he is a member of the California and Florida bars. He received his BA degree from New College of Florida and his law degree, cum laude, from Georgetown University.

Acknowledgments

A grateful thank you to Sarah Orwig, Executive Editor of ABA Publishing, and Michael Beaver and Toni Reed, cochairs of the ABA's Tort Trial and Insurance Practice (TIPS) Publishing Committee, for their guidance and their enthusiastic support of this project. Many thanks as well to my Fisher Phillips partners Jason Geller, Jim Holland, Grace Horoupian, and Jennifer Sandberg and associates Piper Brockley, Chase Dorn, and Patrick Randall for their review of the manuscript of this book and their valuable feedback. The views expressed in this book are solely my own, however.

A Note about Writing Style

I wrote this book in a conversational style to make it an easier and (hopefully) a more enjoyable read than what you usually read in your practice of law. I have used first person, contractions, sentence fragments, some slang, a bit of snark, and more than a few exclamation points. This does not mean that it's OK for you to do the same in your legal writing. Your legal writing must be much more formal and conventional than what you are about to read.

Introduction

So You Want to Be a Star?

Congratulations. Perhaps you have just graduated or you are about to graduate from law school. Or perhaps you already have started working in a law firm and you want some tips on how to get ahead. Either way, you are about to embark on what potentially can be an amazing and rewarding career in law. You have the potential to represent many interesting clients, handle a wide variety of significant legal matters, and even do some good in the world. If you are successful, you will be compensated well for your work, and you could become a leader in your law firm, your community, or beyond. When you are ready to retire, you will look back on your career and likely feel proud of your accomplishments.

Not to put more pressure on you, but how you handle your first few years of law practice can make a lot of difference in how far you will go as a lawyer. My goal for this book is that it will help you make the right moves, and avoid some of the wrong ones, during those important early years on your path to success. If you want to be a star associate in your law firm, keep reading.

For 24 years I managed what has become the largest office in a now-international law firm. I have hired, trained, and mentored dozens of lawyers. I am proud to say that the office I managed has produced many star associates. Most of those associates made partner, and a few even made partner early. Some of those partners have become leaders in the firm, and they are on their way to becoming leaders in the profession. These lawyers love what they do, and they are exceptionally good at it.

During my years of developing and managing lawyers, it has been readily apparent to me which associates "get it" and which do not. The best of the former will become star associates and ultimately partners, and the latter likely will not. So what determines whether a junior lawyer will "get it"?

It's not their choice of law school, because the practice of law is nothing like law school. Graduating from one of the top 20 law schools is not a guarantee of (or prerequisite for) success as a lawyer. There are plenty of lawyers from those top schools who will never "get it," and there are many extraordinarily successful lawyers who attended lower-ranked law schools. Likewise, graduating at the top of your law school class is great, but it will not ensure that you will succeed in a legal career. The legal profession has plenty of summa cum laude law graduates who are not succeeding in the practice of law and can't figure out why.

Most of what makes a lawyer a star involves smart choices, hard work, and the ability to relate to people. You also need skills to succeed in a law firm that you probably did not learn in law school. You can develop those skills, and this book can help you. We will cover a variety of topics, but we'll begin with four key principles that we will touch on from time to time throughout the book:

1. Unless you are an IPO[1] lawyer about to make your client rich, you are probably in the way. We lawyers tend to overestimate our own importance. We think we bring great value to our clients, and often we do. But much of the time we are cleaning up messes, or we are trying to get our clients to follow rules they would rather not follow. Smart lawyers know that our clients are not always our biggest fans. We do not generate revenue for our clients in most instances. We are overhead. Our clients are not nearly as fascinated with the law as we are, moreover. They are focused on making and selling products or providing services in a competitive marketplace. They are under pressure to deliver and to make their numbers. They live in a practical world. They view

1. Initial Public Offering, for you noncorporate types.

legal problems as business problems to be solved, not interesting theories to be pondered or debated. They dislike paying legal bills, and they become impatient when a matter drags on and on. The last thing most of our clients want to hear from their lawyer is "Wow! This case is so interesting it could go all the way to the Supreme Court!"

2. Smart lawyers know they are in the customer service business. The most successful lawyers get to know their clients well and give them what they need, ahead of schedule and under budget. User experience, or UX, has become a popular concept in technology and business, and it applies no less to lawyers and law firms. Lawyers who amass large books of business are adept at providing exceptional UX for their clients. You can do the same. As you gain exposure to the firm's clients, always put yourself in the client's shoes. Return client calls and emails promptly. Clients are not reaching out to you to be sociable. They have a problem or concern that they want your help to resolve. The sooner you address it, the sooner they can move on to something else. Give the client a direct answer, moreover, not an equivocal one. Understand your client, its risk tolerance, and its general approach to resolving problems. When confronted with an advice issue or a strategic decision in litigation, for example, you should carefully evaluate options, present them to the client, and suggest your recommended course of action. Of course, the client ultimately decides on the best option, based on your reasoned and suggested path, but clients do not want you to equivocate. They already know the answer is not clear, or they would not have asked you. If you need more time to find the answer, ask for it. I've never had a client tell me they preferred a quick answer to the right answer. Finally, when sending a client a draft agreement, brief, or discovery responses for review, deliver a high-quality work product well ahead of the deadline, so the client need not rearrange their work priorities or personal time because you were late in sending the document.

3. Partners are busy, so be proactive. Law firm partners are busy people. They must not only produce consistently excellent legal work, but they must also develop and manage client relationships, train and supervise associates, send bills to clients, and get the firm paid. Many partners also have leadership roles in the firm or in the community. They have many priorities competing for their attention. They do not want to have to track down associates to ask them to perform routine tasks or to remind them of deadlines. Partners love associates who anticipate a need and address it (keeping the partner in the loop, of course). Partners much prefer working with an associate who asks, "Should I send out the usual initial written discovery?" or "Should I have subpoenas sent out for the plaintiff's medical records?" than having to ask, "Did we ever send out initial discovery?" or "Where are the plaintiff's medical records?" Partners depend on associates to alert them to coming deadlines in a case or deal. Star associates are proactive. They do not wait to be assigned work. They not only do what is expected of them without being asked, but they also volunteer to take on tasks that might lighten a partner's load, and they alert partners to potential problems or issues in a case or transaction that the partner might not have recognized. Star associates are usually the busiest associates in the firm because partners want to work with associates who make their lives easier.

4. Your reputation is everything. You probably have heard this before, but it bears repeating. Your reputation is the single most valuable asset you will have in the practice of law. Take this very seriously. Your reputation will be based on how you conduct yourself in the legal community and in your firm. Always showing respect for the courts, and showing courtesy and professionalism toward fellow members of the bar, will distinguish you in this "anything goes" era. If your practice takes you to court, learn where to stand and how to address the court, wear a business suit, and be nice to the clerk. Shake hands with your opponent before or after the hearing. Be generous in granting opposing counsel's requests for deadline extensions unless doing so really prejudices your client's interests, because karma is real and your professional courtesies will come back to you. Be true to your word when you negotiate. Within your firm, be honest and forthright with partners and your peers. Don't make excuses or deflect blame. Take responsibility for your actions and admit it if you make a mistake. Meet deadlines, and don't cut corners. Be accessible and responsive. It sounds basic, but many lawyers do not meet these basic standards. Producing great work alone will not move you ahead if you are not viewed as trustworthy and reliable. Also, don't stand out for the wrong reasons. Develop a reputation as an associate who produces excellent work and provides superior client service and not as an associate who requires a lot of management attention for using questionable judgment.

This book will show you how to excel as an associate in a larger law firm. It assumes that your goal is to become a partner in your firm someday, but the techniques we will cover will help you stand out as well if you decide to go in-house, enter government service, or even open your own practice. Excellence will take you to the top no matter which path you choose to pursue in the law. Wherever your career takes you, my hope for you is that you will be one of those lawyers who truly "gets it."

1

First, Get the Job

Whether you are looking for your first job out of law school or for a better opportunity than you currently have, finding the right position requires hard work, preparation, and good judgment. You are not just looking for a job. You are looking for the firm where you can have an extraordinary career. The conventional wisdom is that associates can move from firm to firm early in their careers without affecting their long-term prospects. That's not always true. Too much lateral movement can stall an associate's forward trajectory, so take the time to choose well.

The Right Firm for You

Finding the right firm is a function of understanding yourself and your goals and interests. It requires that you take several factors into consideration. First, what size firm do you want to work for? Do you want to work for a leading global law firm, and do you have the credentials to be hired at such a firm? Such firms offer terrific brands, very sophisticated work, many resources, and relatively generous compensation. There are negatives to working at these firms, however. The work may be sophisticated, but your role in the overall case or project might be small. Such a firm's hours expectations are often substantial, meaning you will be working late nights and weekends. When I was interviewing as a young lawyer at one such firm, one of the first things the firm's recruiter showed me was the room where associates could catch some sleep when working all-nighters. At least they were honest. Partnership opportunities in very large firms can be scarce, too. Associates often leave such firms for smaller firms, in-house positions, or government service. If that is your plan, then such a firm might be right for you, but if your goal is to find a firm where you can make partner, be sure to have a candid discussion with the firm regarding your potential to become a partner someday.

Alternatively, perhaps a smaller national or regional firm, a specialty firm, or a newer but up-and-coming firm might be a better fit for you. You will likely get more hands-on experience early in your career, and you have a better chance at making partner at such a firm. Your salary will be lower than at a larger global firm, but the hours expectation will probably be less. Don't make the mistake of simply picking the highest-paying firm. Manage your personal expenses so you can afford to work at the firm that will provide you with the best opportunity.

Second, you should find a firm that is located where you want to live. If you are single and you want an exciting nightlife and a cosmopolitan lifestyle, you should live in a big city. You will not like living in a suburban environment or a smaller city that closes down by 10 p.m. On the other hand, if you are starting a family and a safe community with good schools is important, living in New York or Los Angeles might not be your best option.[1] Consider home affordability in the area as well if you hope to be a homeowner soon. Also, is it important to you to live close to family? Is a warm climate important, or are cold winters not a concern? Ask yourself these questions because your goal is to find a firm where you can grow and thrive, and for that to occur, you will have to stay a while. Some firms with large office networks might offer the opportunity to switch offices, but if you do so, you will need to

1. You might be thinking, "Well, what about working remotely?" As I explain in Chapter 2, as a junior lawyer you should not work remotely.

become admitted to a new state bar and start over in establishing relationships with partners and peers in your new office. It's better to decide where you want to live before you join a firm.

Third, do you want to practice a particular kind of law? Most lawyers today wind up specializing in an area of law. The only question is whether you will pick your specialty or your firm will pick it for you. If the firm needs securities lawyers, you will become a securities lawyer. If they need products liability defense lawyers, that will become your specialty. Maybe that's fine if you really don't know in which field you want to practice, but if you want to practice intellectual property law or employment law or real estate law, find a firm that has a sophisticated practice in that area and that will allow you to focus on that specialty. A lot of lawyers think they want to be litigators because they look forward to a career filled with courtroom drama. Only a very select few large firm litigators get to try cases, however. Most litigators, even at the partner level, are consumed with pretrial litigation matters such as taking and defending depositions, answering written discovery, and the like. Also, it is sometimes difficult to develop a specialty if you are a litigator in a large firm, which in turn can make it difficult to develop a client base. Many such litigators leave to join a smaller or specialty firm, but often they must learn a new practice area. It can be done, but you will be surrounded by peers who have practiced in that specialty area for much longer than you. It's better to try to take more control over your destiny from the start.

Fourth, pick a firm that aligns with your values. If you have a particular ideological perspective, ask yourself if you will be comfortable doing the work of a firm you are considering. If you cannot imagine yourself working for a firm that defends insurance companies, or manufacturers sued for polluting the environment, or employers accused of sexual harassment, steer clear of those firms. Research the firm carefully and ask questions, should you get an interview, about its practice areas and clients. If you are a racial or ethnic minority or LGBTQ+, explore the firm's commitment to diversity, not just its diversity statement but how it walks the talk. Ask to interview with some of the firm's diverse lawyers to get their perspective. If pro bono work is important to you, find a firm that is committed to pro bono in the way you are. Most firms perform at least some pro bono work, but the types of pro bono work and the amount of credit they give to lawyers doing the work vary.

Fifth, and perhaps most important, select a firm where you think you will feel at home, working with lawyers you like and respect and where you will be valued. When I was searching for my first legal job, I interviewed with some of the top firms in the South, but I had trouble feeling a connection with most of them. One firm looked like the set for a television show. The offices were stunning, and the lawyers and staff were all attractive and well dressed. The firm was a hard-charging new arrival on the scene, but it didn't feel real to me. Another firm was solid and stable, a leader in its community, but it seemed almost *too* stable. I was afraid I would grow restless there. Finally, I happened upon a firm in Atlanta that practiced in an area of law that I liked. Instead of the typical one-day interview including lunch with a partner and an associate, this firm asked me to come to Atlanta and spend the weekend. I interviewed with just about every partner in the firm. One of the senior partners threw a dinner party for me at his home attended by several partners, and his daughter played the harp. I felt they sincerely wanted me to join their firm and, although I had not seriously considered Atlanta as an option, the firm seemed like a great fit. (Forty years later I still think so.) If you have an opportunity to join a firm that sees the star potential in you, you are already on your way.

Writing Your Resume

A well-written resume can help open the right doors for you. A poorly written resume can have the opposite effect. Unless law is your second or third career, you are just starting out in the working world. A resume that consumes more than one page is usually too long. It suggests that you cannot distinguish between what is important and what is not. If your resume takes up more than one page using type no smaller than 11 points, shorten it.

The first thing on your resume should be your objective. Too often, resumes skip the objective and move right to education or employment history. Granted, it might be assumed that you are seeking employment with a law firm, but the reader of your resume will appreciate it if you can narrow your focus. An objective such as "New law graduate with undergraduate degree in engineering seeks opportunity to build a career in intellectual property law with a leading firm in the field" will indicate that you have thought about what you want in your career and that you are looking for more than merely a job.

If you are looking for your first full-time job in law, your next section should be your educational history. If you are looking for a lateral position, your next section should cover your employment history. You want to focus on what is most important to the reader to keep him or her reading.

For your educational history, list your law school, followed by any other colleges and graduate schools you attended. Do not list your high school. If you have come this far, it is assumed that you managed to graduate from high school. The only exception might be if you graduated from an elite prep school where you made connections that could be helpful in your legal career. For your law school, list your year of graduation (or anticipated graduation). Law firm recruiters tend to divide applicants into "classes" based on year of law school graduation. If you are seeking your first job or are in your first few years of practice, include your class rank or grade-point average. Later in your career these measures will be less important, but recruiters of junior lawyers tend to pass over resumes that lack information regarding academic standing in law school.

If you received honors at law school graduation such as "magna cum laude" or "with high honors," list the honors. If you were elected to the Order of the Coif, list it. If you were on law review, include it, and if you wrote a published note or comment, include it too. If you were on the moot court team, include it. If you received a highest-grade award, list it if it seems relevant to the position you are seeking. If I am hiring employment lawyers and you tell me you received the highest-grade award for Trusts and Estates, though, we are wasting time. Include clinics and internships if they are relevant to the position you are seeking. A summer internship at the Securities and Exchange Commission would catch the eye of a recruiter seeking corporate or securities lawyers. A clinic in environmental justice would not. The point is to focus your resume on your qualifications for the opportunity you are seeking, not to list absolutely everything you have done in your life to date.

Similarly, for your pre–law school education, list degrees that you received along with any honors. Be careful not to clutter your resume with details about your prelaw education that are not helpful. If you were selected for Phi Beta Kappa, that's important to include. Your undergraduate sorority or fraternity is less important (unless you know that the managing or hiring partner of the law firm shares the same Greek background). If you played a varsity sport in college, especially on an athletic scholarship, definitely list it because it shows that you are competitive, that you have discipline, and that you are able to succeed in multiple activities simultaneously. If you were student government president, list it. If you received scholarships or fellowships of a substantial nature, include them. Mentions of membership in student organizations or receipt of other awards are less helpful, so you can skip them if you are running short on space.

Include personal details about your college and law school years judiciously. If you started and ran a small business while in college or law school, that will impress a recruiter. If you were a single mother who worked while attending college or law school or you helped to run a family business during school to assist an ailing parent, such experiences tend to show grit that will likely impress a recruiter. Simply working part-time or summers while attending school will not distinguish you, however. Also, details such as that you took off a semester to travel around Europe or that you were president of the sailing club in college are not helpful.

If you are seeking a lateral associate position, your employment history should include all of your full-time positions after law school. Elaborate on your current and prior legal jobs, indicating the areas in which you practiced and tasks you performed, such as drafting agreements, writing summary judgment motions, taking or defending depositions, or second-chairing a trial. Recruiters of lateral lawyers want to hire attorneys with relevant experience. If you worked full time in a judicial clerkship, list it, but stick to the judge, the court, and the dates of the clerkship. Lawyers and legal recruiters know what judicial law clerks do. You do not need to spend two or three lines explaining that you assisted the judge in researching and drafting opinions.

If you held full-time employment between college and law school that involved significant responsibility or achievement, include it. Such jobs would include securities broker, management consultant, human resources manager, engineer, scientist, teacher, accountant, or paralegal. Spend a line or two explaining what you did in those jobs. Jobs such as nanny, retail store employee, or restaurant server should not be included.

If you served in the military, list your branch, your years of service, your final rank, and a brief description of your assignments and responsibilities. Avoid unfamiliar acronyms and military jargon, however, that civilians are unlikely to understand.

Many law students, and even some practicing lawyers, include an interests section on their resume. This is generally a waste of space, however, and it can be counterproductive. Honestly, no one cares if you like yoga, running, hockey, cooking, reading novels, seeing movies, or watching your favorite sports team. If you put something goofy in your interests section, moreover, such as palm reading, bungee jumping, cosplay, or drinking ale in pubs, you'll be judged an unserious person and you will probably not get an interview. I have placed more than a few resumes in the "no" pile based on their listing of peculiar interests. I recognize that some law school career services offices strongly encourage law students to include interests on their resumes. If your law school absolutely insists, and you still have room on your resume to list some interests, go ahead, but stick with a few that will not make it look like you spend your free time exercising poor judgment.

Likewise, the statement "References will be provided upon request" is another complete waste of space. *Of course* you will provide references if we get that far. Law firms are not interested in hiring people who cannot or will not provide references, but you won't get extra points for it.

By no means should you put anything on your resume that is not true. Doing so can get you fired, reported to the state bar, or both. Avoid embellishing your accomplishments too. Experienced readers of resumes can tell when you are trying to make an accomplishment or experience seem like more than it really was. Your credibility is essential in a law firm, and puffery on your resume will get you off on the wrong foot.

Finally, it is sad that I have to say this, but ***proofread your resume!*** There is nothing worse than reading a resume containing typos, misspellings, grammatical errors, inconsistent fonts, and so on. Your resume is your first impression. Submitting a resume with errors makes you look like a careless person. Even one error will make the reader of your resume hesitate to move forward. If you are so careless about your resume, what will your work product look like if we hire you? Set your resume aside for a day or two and then read it again for errors. Have classmates, friends, or relatives read it. Be sure it's perfect before you submit it.

Before you start your job search, don't just update an old resume. Start over. Think about what you should put in your resume to show the reader that you will be a good fit for the position. An important talent for a lawyer is the ability to focus, to eliminate the clutter and get to the point. Start with your resume.

Preparing for the Interview

Good news. You have been invited for one or more interviews. Like almost everything in law, a job interview requires thorough preparation. If you are still in law school and your school offers mock interviews with alumni or other lawyers, you should take advantage of the opportunity to sharpen your interviewing skills in a mock interview. Even if law is not your first career and you have interviewed for jobs before, interviewing for a position in a law firm is different than interviews for other types of jobs, so you would likely benefit from a mock interview.

Once you have honed your interview skills a bit, you will be ready to prepare for an interview with a specific law firm. The most impressive interviewee is the one who is conversant with the law firm conducting the interview. It shows the candidate's interest in the firm, and it makes it easier during the interview to move past the basics to more meaningful topics.

First, research the firm if you have not already done so. The firm's website is a good place to start. Learn the firm's practice areas, the industries it serves, and its office locations. Read the firm's client alerts or insights posted on its website to get an idea of the firm's real focus in its practice. Focus especially on any client alerts or insights covering the practice area in which you hope to work, and take note of the authors. Google the firm as well to find news of major cases or transactions handled, new office locations, acquisitions of other firms, and the like.

Second, ask the recruiter for a list of attorneys with whom you will be interviewing and read the firm website bio for each attorney. If you cannot get such a list, read the bios of the office managing partner, the office recruiting partner (if indicated), and the lawyers in the office who practice in your area of focus. Chances are that most of your interviews will be with these people. Take note of where each went to college and law school, to see if you went to the same schools. Read about their practices; most law firm bios cover the lawyers' areas of practice and important accomplishments. Also look at any leadership positions the lawyer has held in the community. Look for ways to relate to the lawyers who will be interviewing you. Saying something like "I read in your bio that you won the trial in the *Snorkheim* case; I worked on a similar case in my current firm last year" or "I read the article you wrote on how AI might impact client hiring practices" will make you more relatable to the interviewer than simply asking her to describe her practice. Make a list of likely interviewers and note at least one relatable topic you can discuss with each.

Third, consider your personal appearance. Do you need a haircut before the interview? Do you need to get a suit cleaned? Unless a firm representative tells you to dress in business casual attire, wear a business suit, including a tie for men. If the interview is to be conducted remotely, be sure you have an adequate webcam, adequate lighting, and a professional-looking background for the interview. Do not attempt to do an interview with your cell phone, and be sure you will have a space available for you to do the interview without background noise or interruptions by roommates, family members, or pets.

Finally, make a list of questions you will want to ask during the interview. Examples of such questions are in the next section. You will want to structure your time so you can establish rapport with the interviewer, answer his or her questions of you, and ask the questions you have within the allotted interview time. The more organized you are, the better you will perform.

The Interview

On the day of the interview, give yourself plenty of time to travel to the firm's office location. Allow time for traffic and for finding parking. Showing up late and blaming traffic leaves a terrible first impression.

Introduce yourself to each interviewer with a firm handshake and look him or her in the eye as you introduce yourself. Unless it's obvious where you are supposed to sit, wait for the interviewer to direct you.

Sometimes the interviewer will start by peppering you with specific questions. Other times the interviewer will start with an open-ended question such as "Tell me about yourself" or "Why are you interested in joining our law firm?" Be ready to respond to these questions. You might get the question "Why did you decide to become a lawyer?" Avoid cliché answers such as "I like helping people" or "I want to pursue justice." Instead, provide an authentic answer that accurately describes why you chose this profession. Importantly, do your best to address the questions you are asked. While you might be nervous, resist the temptation to get too far off track in responding.

When it is your turn to ask questions, make good use of your time both to get the information you need and to make a good impression. First, ask a question or two, as suggested in the previous section, to establish rapport with the interviewer. Find some common ground, if you can, regarding schools attended, matters handled, articles written, or community involvement. If you cannot establish common ground, ask the interviewer a question about an accomplishment or leadership position listed in his web bio, such as "Did you find that being on the board of the chamber of commerce was helpful in developing clients?"

After establishing rapport with the interviewer, ask questions that demonstrate your interest in the firm as potentially the place to pursue your legal career. Some examples:

- How does mentoring of associates occur in your firm?
- What kind of work should I expect to perform as a new associate?
- Tell me about the types of clients your firm represents.
- If I was working directly with you on a case, how could we best work together?
- How much client contact do junior associates have at this firm?
- How does the firm evaluate whether junior associates are performing satisfactorily?

- If I was to join this firm, what potential might I have to become a partner someday?
- At what point are associates expected to begin generating their own business?
- What opportunities might I have to work with partners and associates in other offices of the firm?
- Does this firm encourage its associates to become involved in the community?
- How can I make the greatest contribution to the firm as a junior associate?

If you interview with any associates, especially junior associates, ask some of the following questions:

- Is there a formal mentoring program here? If not, how does mentoring work?
- How are junior associates evaluated here?
- What kinds of work do you perform besides research and drafting?
- Do you have contact with the firm's clients?
- What is the "official" billable hours requirement, and is there a different actual requirement?
- Do you feel that you have the potential to make partner here?
- What made you choose to work at this firm?
- If you could change one thing about this firm, what would it be?

Avoid asking questions about associate pay during these interviews. You should have received salary range information from the recruiter, the job posting, or the law firm's recruiting materials at your law school. Also, avoid asking questions about how much vacation is offered or about "work-life balance" at the firm. Others might disagree with me on this point, but my experience has been that candidates who ask about these topics up front can give the impression that they lack the work ethic required to succeed at the firm. Should you receive an offer, it will be appropriate at that time to ask about salary, bonuses, vacation, paid leave time, and other benefits. At the interview stage, however, you will want to show the firm that your primary interest is in advancing your career, not in planning your time off.

The Interview Meal

Some interviews are conducted over breakfast, lunch, or dinner. The purpose of doing so is to put the candidate in a less formal setting to get to know him or her better. People tend to let their guard down a bit more in social settings. You will want to relax and not be too stiff and formal at an interview meal, but be careful what you reveal about yourself. Because an interview over a meal is usually longer than an office interview, there is more time for the interviewers to ask you questions about your personal background, interests, hobbies, and so on. It is important that you be genuine in your responses and allow the interviewers to get to know you as a person, but do not introduce awkward topics such as recent deaths or serious illnesses in your family or marital or relationship problems you are having. You also should avoid talking about politics or about any political campaigns or activities in which you are involved. Lawyers fall all along the political spectrum, and most law firms contain a mix of conservatives and liberals, Democrats and Republicans. You don't want to start a political debate during a job interview.

What you choose to eat during an interview over a meal is reflective of your judgment. The primary purpose of the interview meal is to interview, not to eat. Avoiding messy foods like pasta and loaded cheeseburgers should be obvious, but you will want to order food that comes in a small portion and is easy to eat, so that you will not be so busy feeding yourself that you cannot participate in the conversation. Alcohol consumption over lunch is uncommon today, but alcohol might be offered over dinner. If you do not drink, or you have difficulty handling your alcohol, politely decline. If you decide to have a drink, stick to something safe like a glass of wine and limit yourself to one. In addition to being hospitable, your hosts are testing your judgment and seeing how you engage in a social environment.

Finally, handle any mishaps that might occur during the meal calmly and gracefully. If the server brings you the wrong entrée, or it is cold, or someone spills their iced tea on you, take it in stride.

Do not become angry or confrontational. Consider it the first of many tests of how you will handle the stress you will experience over the course of your legal career.

After the Interview

Your law school probably told you to send a thank-you note to each interviewer after the interview. Whether you send an email or a handwritten note, make your message personal and authentic. If you handwrite a thank-you note, use nice, personalized stationery. Consider starting the note with something other than "Thank you . . ." Start instead with something more engaging, such as "I appreciate your taking the time to meet with me and sharing your approach to mentoring associates. I know I would benefit from your approach." Even more impactful is when you write a note or email to the interviewer showing that you did some brief research on a topic discussed during the interview. Something like "I enjoyed our discussion of the *Snorkheim* case. I did some research and found that in *Gersten v. Nortco Enterprises*, the appellate court last month affirmed the same result as in *Snorkheim*. I'm sure you are aware of it, but I found the appellate court's opinion to be very persuasive and I attach a copy." Partners like it when associates show initiative. When *prospective* associates show initiative, partners know that you get it.

The Job Offer and Your Response

Good for you. You got the offer. Be sure to get all of the details now—salary, bonus eligibility, when salaries are reevaluated, vacation and leave policies, health insurance, 401(k), and bar exam leave and expense reimbursement if applicable. You will likely get a formal offer letter. If anything is unclear, by all means seek clarification. Once you understand the offer, you must decide whether to accept it, reject it, or attempt to negotiate it.

Negotiation can be risky. Sometimes, experienced senior associates in a tight labor market can negotiate an increase in the salary offered or a signing bonus, but it is rare that recent law graduates and junior associates are able to do so. If you try, you run the risk of giving the impression that you are dissatisfied before you even get started. It is better to decline the offer and find a firm that can pay you what you need.

If you need time off a few months after your start date for a wedding and honeymoon or other important life event, mention it when you receive your offer. Firms will not deny you the time off, and they will appreciate your notifying them in advance. If you are a lateral associate and you want to take some time off before starting a new job, most firms will be accommodating. If you are a new lawyer starting your first job, however, avoid asking for a different start date. Most firms have all of their new law graduates start on the same date so the onboarding and orientation process can proceed in an orderly fashion.

When you are sure of your decision to join the law firm, communicate your acceptance of the offer in writing, and prepare yourself for this important career move.

2

Show Up for the Job

It's your first day on the job in your new firm. Know where and when you are expected to show up and show up a bit early. If you drive, allow for extra time for traffic and for navigating an unfamiliar area, and allow for time to find where you are supposed to park.

Once you have arrived at the office, you will be introduced to many people and forget most of their names. You will complete dozens of forms and documents in order to get paid, receive benefits, be listed in firm directories, and so on. You will meet your legal assistant, who will seem very busy, and you will wonder if he or she will have enough bandwidth to assist you. You will view countless online training presentations. All of this is called "onboarding and orientation," and it will be your first opportunity to engage and make a good impression.

When onboarding and orientation are finished, you will be ready for work assignments. A few days might go by before you get any assignments, but don't worry. It might take some time, especially if you are still awaiting your bar exam results. The work will come.

Go into the Office

The COVID pandemic showed us that we can work from just about anywhere there is an adequate Wi-Fi connection. Zoom and Teams were not invented during COVID, but the pandemic made us take notice of them. Many attorneys spent their days during the pandemic in front of their computer screens and web-cams, meeting with clients, opposing counsel, mediators, even judges. Never again would an attorney in a major city have to drive two hours or more each way to take a deposition or participate in a mediation. With their daily commute eliminated as well, many attorneys became more productive. They also had flexibility to take care of children at a time when commercial child care was scarce, and they found they had to spend far less money on business attire, gas, parking, and lunch.

Working from home quickly became a popular thing in law firms as well as in many other businesses. Some attorneys took the opportunity to move out of urban areas and even to other states in search of a better life. After the pandemic subsided, most firms attempted to get their attorneys to return to the office, but more than a few of those attorneys resisted. At the same time, some firms saw an opportunity to shed some expensive office space. If most attorneys show up only a couple of times per week, if at all, why not move to a "hoteling" arrangement and save some money on real estate?

Remote work is here to stay. It's just too beneficial to too many people. Recognizing this, some firms have moved to a hybrid approach that requires attorneys to be in the office two or three days per week. The thinking has been that on the days when attorneys are in the office, they can collaborate, network, give and receive mentoring, and meet in person concerning work assignments. The arrangement sounds good in theory, but law practice is still a five-day-a-week (at a minimum) occupation. Clients do not need legal advice only on Tuesdays and Wednesdays. Associates sometimes get stuck on an assignment and need to confer with a colleague or a partner on a Monday, Thursday, or Friday. Friday's new opportunity will not wait until next Tuesday for a response.

Some partners might follow the hybrid schedule, others might not, depending on court calendars and client demands. Some partners might still show up in the office every day because that is how they have become accustomed to working and it has made them very successful. If you are a junior associate, you need to be in the office when partners are there. No matter that your firm might have teams or clusters to help direct work assignments, many partners still assign work by walking down the hall and finding the first associate who does not look too busy. You will miss out if you are not in the office when this occurs. One rising star associate in my firm not only showed up to work in the office every day during her first year, but she also placed a bowl of wrapped chocolates on her desk for visitors. Attorneys from all over our suite stopped by her office for a chocolate. She turned out to be the busiest associate in her first-year class, and with her entrepreneurial thinking she is likely to go far.

Even if partners are away from the office, you still need to be in the office. Partners will call your office number with a new opportunity but will be less inclined to look up your cell phone number to chase you down if you are not in the office. True, technology exists to forward calls to your laptop computer or your cell phone, but it works only if you take time to connect it. Even if it works, if you are out walking the dog when the partner calls, you might still miss out on the opportunity.

Being in the office also fosters collaboration with your colleagues. Much of the process of learning the practice of law comes from sharing problems and solutions with other lawyers in your firm. If you are a junior associate having difficulty with an issue, it's easy to walk down the hall to a fellow associate to seek help. It can be more difficult to locate such a colleague when everyone is working remotely, even if you have a current list of everyone's cell phone numbers or you are able to message colleagues on Teams or a similar messaging platform. Also, it can be more difficult to call or message someone not knowing if you are interrupting something important than it is to peek inside their office.

Likewise, learning the practice of law is an apprenticeship, which will be addressed in more detail later in this chapter. It involves learning by observing partners and senior associates and then learning by doing. You cannot readily learn in this fashion if you are working at home.

Finally, your mental health might well depend on your showing up in the office for work every day. Working remotely can be an isolating experience, especially if you moved to a new city to begin your career and you have not yet developed a local social network. It is important to be around other people when you are in a new environment. In addition, the first few years of law practice are a stressful time. You will be faced with many new challenges as you learn the law in your specialty field and learn the craft of practicing law. In many cases you will need to surmount these challenges quickly in order to meet deadlines. When you are working at home alone, the stress of dealing with these challenges can be overwhelming. When you are around other associates who are dealing with the same challenges, the stress is much easier to handle.

For all of these reasons, new law graduates should work in the office every day during at least the first three years of practice, and new lateral attorneys should work in the office daily for at least a year after joining a new firm. The career benefits of doing so far outweigh the comfort and convenience of working remotely. Keep this in mind when choosing a place to live as you start your new law firm job. Choose a manageable commute or proximity to public transportation.

I know, there will be days when you just cannot resist working from home. You will justify it because the partners with whom you work are all away, or you are a bit under the weather, or the guy is coming to fix your refrigerator. On the rare occasions that you work from home, be sure you have the right equipment. You will need a reliable Wi-Fi connection so that you can connect to your firm's network and a good webcam and headset or speakers in case you are pulled into a Zoom or Teams meeting. If you do participate in a videoconference, dress professionally. A business suit is not necessary, but a dress shirt or blouse is far preferable to gym clothes or a hoodie. And be cognizant of the background behind you. If it does not look professional, use a virtual background that looks businesslike, not a scene of the beach or the wine country.

Your Own Personal Office

If your firm is not committed to "hoteling," you will probably be assigned your own personal office. The appearance of your office will reflect your personality but also your judgment and discipline. Of course, you may decorate it with photos of your passions, your adventures, people who are important to you, and even your pets if you like. If you have an autographed photo of your favorite pro athlete, musician, or other public figure, display it (assuming the public figure is not too polarizing). If you have an autographed football or basketball you wish to put in your office to show your interest in the sport, go ahead. One of my associates has a field hockey stick hanging in her office, which tends to stimulate conversation about that sport.

Hang your law degree and college diploma in your office if you desire. Hang some tasteful art if you are so inclined. Hang your child's watercolor paintings too. Just be sure your office décor does not look too cluttered, and avoid hanging or displaying items that look tacky or that might generate controversy.

Keep your office looking neat and orderly, and if you have a guest chair or chairs, keep them clear of books and papers so that visitors to your office might sit and chat with you for a moment. You will likely find some partners' offices stacked high with files and with books and papers strewn everywhere. When you are a partner you can have a messy office too, but until then understand that an orderly office will reflect a disciplined mind.

Finally, be careful not to leave confidential or sensitive documents out in the open in your office overnight or when you are away traveling or on vacation. Lock all such items away in your desk or file cabinet before you leave, and if you discard sensitive items, put them in a shredder and not in your office wastebasket.

Dressing the Part

A generation ago, dressing for law practice was easy. You wore a business suit every day. Even if you never left the office and did not see a client, you still wore a suit.

That all has changed, of course. "Business casual," which has about as many meanings as wearers, has become appropriate for many, *but not all*, settings. It is never appropriate for court or other adversarial proceedings. Those still require a business suit. I do not think it is appropriate for depositions or mediations, either, but I recognize that others have a different view.

For client settings it just depends. If a partner asks you to join a meeting in the office with a client, or to visit a client, ask about appropriate attire. Some clients expect their lawyers to dress up even if they do not. Other clients are more comfortable if their lawyers dress like them. If you are going to visit a client in an industrial setting, dressing down is more acceptable than if you visit a client that is a bank. When in doubt, wear a suit. If you are overdressed, next time dress more casually. That's better than being the only person dressed casually in a room full of suits.

If you wear business casual attire to the office, remember the *business* part of the term. Generally, that means a long-sleeve shirt and chino-type trousers for men and a similar look or a casual dress or pantsuit for women. It's always a good idea to keep a blue or black blazer hanging on the back of your office door. Wear loafers or casual lace-up shoes. Don't wear sneakers, particularly bright-colored ones. You never know when a key client might be visiting the office and wanting to meet with you briefly for an update on the case you are handling. You do not want to show up for such a meeting wearing bright-colored sneakers (unless your client makes sneakers and you are wearing the brand).

Some firms have "casual Fridays" that allow for jeans and sweatshirts and similar attire. Do not partake if you know you will be meeting with a client in the office or virtually. Even if you wear jeans, be ready to pivot to a dressier look in case of an unexpected client meeting. Put on a long-sleeve shirt and that blazer hanging on the back of your door.

Regardless of the acceptable mode of dress for the day at the office, avoid wearing T-shirts, hoodies, ripped jeans, hats, flip-flops, and the like. You are not at home or with your friends on the weekend. You are at work in a profession where clients seek your advice and assistance on important matters. Imagine you are about to be wheeled into surgery and your surgeon shows up wearing tattered jeans, sandals, a rock band T-shirt, and a ball cap on backward. Your client will be thinking the same thing if you dress that way.

When at the office or around clients, don't let your attire become a source of distraction. If you can afford expensive designer clothing, shoes, and accessories, good for you. It's probably best to save them for special events, though. The same goes for expensive watches and flashy jewelry. Consider your audience if you are contemplating wearing designer clothing or expensive jewelry to work. Doing so might not fit well in a client setting, unless the client is in the fashion or jewelry business. In the office it could cause some of your peers or some staff to become uncomfortable or even resentful, and that will be counterproductive because you will likely need them as allies. Once you make partner you will be free to develop your own brand, which might include dressing in designer clothing and wearing expensive jewelry. On your way up the ladder, however, you will want people focusing on your legal skills and not on your wardrobe.

Learning the Ropes

Similar to the way you dress at the firm, you will not want to stand out as the square peg in a firm of round holes. This should not require great moral compromise on your part, only that you pay attention to the firm's rules and procedures.

The orientation that you will receive in your first few days should teach you a lot. One of the most important tasks to learn is how to record your time. Billable attorney time is what creates revenue for the law firm, so most firms take timekeeping very seriously. Know the deadline for when you must have your time entered, but if possible you should enter all of your time for a given day before you leave work that day. The longer you wait to enter your time, the more likely you are to forget to bill for a particular task. Be sure to learn how to find and include the correct client and matter codes for each time entry. Also learn how to write time entries that the billing partner will not have to rewrite and the client will not refuse to pay for. Many firms provide training on writing billing entries. If your firm does, take it. (We'll cover this more in Chapter 3, too.)

Know your firm's billable hours expectation for associates. Many firms will give you credit for valuable but nonbillable time such as training time, client development, pro bono work, and so on, so know what you can get credit for and how to record the time. Some firms provide lower billable hours goals for first-year associates with the expectation that you will spend substantial time on nonbillable work and training. Again, know what your targets are, and over the course of the year keep up with your progress toward meeting your targets.

On the topic of billable time, *never, ever* intentionally pad your time. I do not mean here that you simply took too long to complete an assignment. That is common among junior associates. If it happens, record all of your time and let the billing partner decide how much of it to bill. I also don't mean you should sit up at night worrying that you recorded 0.5 of an hour for a client call when on second thought it might have only lasted 0.4. What I mean is that you must never record time that you know you did not work. You must not record four hours for a project when you know you only worked two hours, for example. Doing so is unethical and potentially criminal. If you are caught (and law firms have ways of catching it), you will be fired and possibly disbarred.

Another important subject to learn as part of your orientation is your firm's information technology (IT) and data security policies. Law firms are common targets of malicious online actors, and most firms have heavily fortified their defenses. Unfortunately, these defenses impose some inconvenience on attorneys and other firm users. For example, you will typically have to complete a two-factor authentication to access your firm's IT system or certain data on the system. Never try to shortcut or end-run the firm's IT security procedures, however. Also, pay attention to the firm's rules concerning what you can and cannot do with your firm computer. Many firms have rules against inserting unapproved USB drives into your computer or using an unapproved document sharing portal to send or receive large electronic document files from outside the firm. Most firms have rules regarding installation of outside programs on your firm computer and what to do if you suspect you have received a "phishing" email. Be sure you are familiar with these rules and comply with them. You do not want to be known as the associate who caused your firm to suffer a massive data breach.

Learn your firm's policies regarding use of electronic research tools such as Westlaw and Lexis. Is unlimited use of these tools permitted, or is use limited to billable projects? Learn what other research tools your firm has available, such as electronic libraries of treatises and practice manuals that you can access from your computer. Bookmark these resources in your web browser so you can access them quickly. Also learn about your firm's policy on using generative artificial intelligence (AI) applications such as ChatGPT and AI-based legal research tools to assist with legal research.

You should additionally familiarize yourself with your firm's policies regarding mandatory continuing legal education (MCLE). Some firms have extensive internal MCLE libraries. Other firms provide each attorney an allowance for outside MCLE courses.

If you practice in a state that requires MCLE, know the number of hours you need to complete and by when. Attorneys can have their licenses suspended for not keeping up with their MCLE requirements.

Finally, you should become familiar with your firm's policy for reimbursing business expenses, business travel, and client entertainment. Before you go buying a docking station and dual monitors so you can work from home, know whether your firm will reimburse you (and remember, it's best not to be working from home in the first place). Know when your firm will reimburse mileage and parking so you do not submit expenses that are not allowed. If you will travel on business, know your firm's guidelines for purchasing airline tickets, reserving rental cars, selecting hotels, and reimbursement of meals and other expenses while traveling. Don't be the associate who flew first class, rented a sporty convertible, and stayed the weekend at a nice resort at the firm's expense on your first business trip. Also, learn what is allowed in terms of client meals and entertainment. Most firms will happily reimburse lunch or coffee with clients or genuine prospects, but you should not try to obtain reimbursement for an expensive dinner with four of your law school classmates and their spouses on the theory that they might go in-house someday and possibly hire your firm. That sort of thing invites the wrong kind of attention from your office's managing partner.

Recognize That You Are an Apprentice

The way new lawyers are trained in the United States is a bit peculiar. Upon passing the bar exam, a new lawyer is assumed to be competent to perform every legal service and appear in just about every court in the state on behalf of clients. New law graduates know next to nothing about how to practice law, however. Unless they took a clinical course in law school, their practical experience is usually limited to having argued a (pretend) case before three (pretend) appellate judges in moot court.

Few other professions treat their new members this way. New doctors must complete a residency where they learn the practice of medicine on real patients. New architects typically do a "co-op" with an architecture firm before practicing on their own. Electricians, plumbers, carpenters, and other skilled tradespersons must complete an apprenticeship before becoming a journeyman. Lawyers in Canada must complete a year of "articling" before being admitted to practice, which involves working essentially as a law clerk in a law firm under the supervision of a senior lawyer.

The practical reality in the United States is that most new lawyers also must complete an apprenticeship to become qualified to practice law. It does not have that title and the process is not as formalized as in other professions, but it exists nonetheless. Recognize, therefore, that in your first few years of practice you will be an apprentice lawyer, learning the craft of lawyering under the supervision of partners and other senior lawyers. Some junior associates resist this. "I have my bar license! What more do I need?" They need a lot, and with the attitude that they have nothing left to learn after passing the bar exam, new lawyers are likely to fail.

So how do you be an apprentice lawyer? You learn by watching, and then by doing. By watching, I mean you observe more senior lawyers engaged in the actual practice of law. You watch them give advice to clients, you watch them take depositions, you watch them argue in court, you watch them negotiate complex transactions or settlements of cases. While you are watching senior colleagues practicing law, listen to them carefully as well. Pay attention to the words they use and how they use them. You will notice that the most accomplished lawyers speak very clearly and with a minimum of jargon.

Many larger firms have formalized training programs for junior associates, but you still might have to take some initiative during your apprenticeship years to be able to observe senior lawyers in the practice of law. Ask partners and senior associates if you can observe their depositions, negotiations, and court appearances.

Ask if you can be a junior member of a deal team. They will almost always welcome you (and if they don't, it's probably because of a difficult client relationship, so don't take it personally).

Likewise, ask for opportunities to do the first draft of a contract, write a response to a demand letter, answer discovery, take the deposition of a nonparty witness, or argue a motion in court. Before partners will allow you to have this kind of responsibility, however, they must be confident that you are ready. They are not willing to risk a key client relationship on your not being ready. "OK," you say. "How will they know I am ready if I have not yet done these things?" There is no clear marker that indicates you are ready. Rather, it is a sense that a partner develops from observing your mastery of basic skills such as writing research memos or other written work product, as well as less tangible qualities such as your presence and availability, your professionalism, your responsiveness, whether you have met assigned deadlines, and how you have interacted with clients when given the opportunity. In other words, how well you seem to "get it" so far.

When you are given the opportunity to step up and perform a new task, give it your absolute best. Don't be so consumed with other projects that you cannot devote the time necessary to do the best possible job on the new assignment entrusted to you by a partner. Work nights and weekends if necessary to ensure that you have provided the best possible work product or that you are thoroughly prepared to conduct the deposition or hearing. You will be nervous, and you will make mistakes.[2] All beginners do. But if you give it your best, it should turn out OK.

A critical skill you must learn as a lawyer is how to give advice to a client. Law school actually set you back in this regard because it highlighted the arguments on both sides of every issue. Clients

2. When entrusted to take my first deposition as a junior associate, I commenced the deposition by spilling an entire pitcher of ice water on the court reporter and myself. The world did not end, however. After we cleaned up the mess, the deposition proceeded, and I went on to win my first motion for summary judgment.

don't want that. They want a real answer. They understand there is risk. They incur risk every day when they open the doors of their business. They want you to give them practical advice on how to mitigate that risk based on your understanding of where the law is today and where the law might go tomorrow. This is one of the hardest things you will do as you develop as a lawyer. You can make it easier by observing partners as they advise clients. You will see that the advice is practical and to the point. Not "the court's majority said this but the dissenters said that, and it will all likely have to go back to the court again for clarification." To the contrary, the partner lays out the legal risks of each potential move and lets the client make the business decision about what they want to do. Alternatively, the client might ask for a recommendation, and the partner provides one, along with the rationale. These are the interactions between lawyer and client that lead to the lawyer developing a relationship as a trusted advisor to the client. Once established, these relationships can last for decades, and it is how partners develop their books of business. You should try to observe the process as much as you can during your apprenticeship years.

Another important skill you must learn as an apprentice lawyer is how and where to find the answer to the client's question efficiently. We will address this topic in more detail in the next chapter, but unlike in law school when you had almost limitless time to research an answer to a question, in real-life practice you must find the answer quickly. The client cannot wait for days and will not pay for hours of your reading case law on every question they pose. Finding the right answer efficiently will become easier as you learn a specialty area because there are certain basic rules that govern most specialty areas of the law. These basic rules will get you started. Even if you have learned the basic rules, though, it will not likely be enough to answer the client's question. You must become accustomed to the research tools available inside and outside your firm that can help focus your search for the right answer. If you are not yet familiar with those tools, ask a partner or two in your practice area about their three most useful tools for finding answers to client questions.

Take advantage of your apprenticeship years as a chance to learn as much as you can about the law and the practice of law. One of my mentors when I was a junior associate told me to focus on learning as much as I could during my first three years of practice, because after those three years things start happening so fast that there is much less time for learning. It turned out he was correct.

Build Relationships with Your Peers

Your success as a law firm associate will depend in part on your ability to build relationships with your peers. It is important to be connected with the associates in your entering class (or at least some of them if the class is large), so you can compare notes and common experiences. If you have difficulty with the firm's timekeeping system, for example, you can probably find a classmate who has mastered it to show you how. You should stay in regular touch with these associates, perhaps meeting for coffee or lunch on a regular basis. Much of what you will face in your new law firm will be unfamiliar, but with the mutual support of your fellow incoming associates, it will not seem so intimidating.

You should also connect with an associate or two who are a year ahead of you. They went through what you are going through only last year, so their experience and perspectives will be fresh. When it comes to working with a particular partner, ask a more senior associate who has worked with that partner what the partner prefers in terms of written work product or whether the partner is OK with your contacting the client on your own. Each partner has developed a distinct style of practice that has been successful for him or her. Rely on your more senior colleagues to help you learn about that practice style so you are not always swimming upstream when working with the partner.

Find Mentors

Your firm might have a formal mentoring program where you are assigned to a partner or senior associate as your mentor. You should connect with your mentor and participate in the mentoring program. Use your assigned mentor as a resource for questions you have about firm policies and procedures. Also go to your mentor if you are having difficulty working with a partner and need some advice on how to handle the situation or if you are having issues with your assistant or other support staff.

You will need as many mentors as you can find, however, so don't stop with your assigned mentor. Find your own mentors as well. You might find that you are working for some partners more than others. If you get along well with them, adopt one or two as informal mentors. Also look for mentors with whom you have something in common, such as the same college or law school, the same race or ethnicity or sexual orientation, or the same background before becoming a lawyer. Look for role model mentors as well, such as a partner who has developed a unique practice area that you like or who has balanced a successful career with raising children. Senior associates can be great mentors as well. Star associates tend to be leaders among their peers, and they are role models you will want to get to know. Identify a star associate or two a few classes ahead of you and see if you can establish a mentoring relationship with them.

Your mentors may seem very busy, but connect with them anyway. They generally will make time for you if you seek them out. Use your time with them efficiently to seek their guidance with issues you might have regarding your career development, work-life balance, working with particular partners, or learning a new skill in the practice of law. With respect to both formal and informal mentors, moreover, solicit feedback from them. Ask them how they think you are doing generally or whether they think you handled a particular situation well. Mentors don't want to just walk in cold and give you unsolicited advice, so make it a two-way conversation.

Work with as Many Partners as You Can

You should try to work with as many partners in your practice area as you can. If there are only a few partners in your practice area in your office, look for opportunities to work with partners in other offices too. There are two reasons for this.

First, you will find that each partner has a different style of practicing law. It's not that some are right and others wrong; they are just different. Some pursue a "scorched earth" approach to litigation. Others pick their battles more selectively and try to maintain good relations with opposing counsel. Some prepare obsessively for depositions, hearings, and trials. Others take a bigger-picture approach and prefer compact outlines over detailed scripts. Each partner will prepare a witness differently. Each partner will negotiate a settlement or transaction differently. Some partners might make detailed notes about every client conference they have. Others might just scribble a few key points on a legal pad. Some partners will draft and redraft a brief or agreement, then redraft it several more times. Others will start with an outline and produce no more than a couple of drafts. Some partners will be excitable and frenetic, others more chill. By exposing yourself to different work styles you will begin to adopt a work style that is comfortable for you. Also, by working with different partners you will learn more about their subspecialty areas. You will find some subspecialty areas to be intriguing and others not so much.

Second, the more positive experiences you have working with different partners, the more supporters you will have when it is time for you to advance in status in the firm and eventually move into partnership. Most firms have a formal system of evaluating associates' work performance. Several partners singing your praises will always be more beneficial than just one or two partners. Even outside of the formal evaluation system, partners talk with each other about their experiences with associates. The more partners you have talking you up, the more partners there will be who will want to work with you.

Respect the Support Staff

Support staff in a law firm are to junior associates what senior noncommissioned officers are to junior commissioned officers in the military. Sure, you outrank them, but if you listen to them and respect them, they'll help prevent you from getting yourself killed or at least from committing errors that might jeopardize your career.

First of all, law firms will not tolerate associates abusing staff. Excellent support staff are hard to find, and they will not stay at a firm where they are treated poorly. Yelling at your assistant or calling the IT guy a moron will likely get you an appointment with human resources. You must do more than control your temper, though. You must be considerate of the support staff, especially your assistant. Gone are the days when some lawyers had their own assistant and maybe two lawyers at most would share an assistant. Now, your assistant might be supporting five or more lawyers, and all of them are likely to be senior to you. That does not mean your assistant will never be able to help you, but you must plan ahead. You cannot drop a major filing on your assistant's desk at 4:30 p.m. when she must leave work at 5 p.m. to pick up her kids. If you have a major filing due, talk with your assistant in advance to learn when you will need to have it ready. You might consider holding a short weekly meeting with your assistant to go over the projects you will need assistance with over the next week. This will help avoid last-minute surprises.

Second, recognize that your assistant and your paralegal (if you work with one) already know more than you will learn in a long time about how law is actually practiced. They know how court filings must be formatted, which documents must be included, which documents must be filed electronically, and which must be hand-delivered to the court. They know the competent court reporters, process servers, and investigators. They know how to get favors from court clerks when you need them, and they can get information from a court clerk that the clerk will not tell you. They have seen lawyers make a lot of mistakes, so they will know when you are about to make one. If your assistant or paralegal tells you that you are doing something wrong, you probably are. Your assistant and paralegal are extremely valuable resources for you. Treat them accordingly. In addition to showing respect and consideration, birthday flowers or wine and an occasional gift card go a long way.

Third, recognize as well that your firm's support staff are not as intense about the practice of law as you are. Many of them are hourly employees who look forward to clocking out at the end of the day and having a life, whether it involves spending time with family, pursuing hobbies or interests, or even running a side business. Most law firm staff are highly competent and conscientious about their work, but it is not their only focus in life. Many of them could have gone to law school, and some of them probably did but chose not to practice because they had different priorities. They will give you the support you need, but they will not be keen to work until midnight or on Sunday afternoon.

Make good use of the time your assistant has for you, therefore. Focus your assistant on the important things like properly formatting your documents, filing your pleadings, and scheduling your depositions. Do your own expense reports and make your own travel arrangements. I know that runs counter to most lawyers' habits, but it's your money and your trip. I learned my lesson with respect to travel arrangements when I arrived at the airport one day for an important trip only to find that my assistant had booked me on the next day's flight. If you want to be sure you will be on the flight you need and that a hotel room will be waiting for you when you arrive, book them yourself and double-check the confirmations when you receive them.

Finally, know that staff talk about associates with each other and with partners, who typically value their opinions. Partners listen to what staff have to say about associates because staff's impression of an associate is likely to be similar to a client's impression of an associate. You want your firm's staff to be saying good things about you.

What should you do if your assistant really is incompetent or simply does not have time for you? Talk with your office administrator, your mentor, or a supervising partner. Sometimes it's just not a good fit. If you have been respectful toward your assistant and are reasonable in your expectations, firm administration will try to find another solution for you. Speak up, though, when you know there is a problem. Do not wait until an assistant who is overworked or simply not up to the task makes a serious mistake on your behalf.

3

Doing the Work

Now that you're settled in at the firm, it's time to get to work. Your initial work assignments as a new lawyer will likely be a mix of some document review and some research assignments. Once you receive your bar exam results and are admitted to the bar, you might be assigned to draft responses to discovery, draft motions and supporting or opposition papers, or draft or respond to demand letters. As you demonstrate your proficiency at one task, you will be given another to further develop your skills as a lawyer. First, though, you must master the foundational skills of researching and analyzing the law.

Performing Legal Analysis

In law school you primarily studied casebooks that presented excerpts of various cases and other materials relevant to the topics covered in the course. With the possible exception of your legal writing course or a clinical course, you were not presented with a problem and told to go out into the legal world and find the solution. That is what you will do throughout your career as a lawyer, however, so you will need to learn how to do it well.

The legal questions you will be assigned to research will not have obvious answers. If they did, a client would not be paying your firm for you to do the research. If you think you found the right answer quickly, you probably didn't. You likely missed something, or the case you found on point was later reversed or overruled.[3]

Rather, you must locate statutes, regulations, and case authority from which you might find the answer through the process of legal analysis. You learned about statutes, regulations, and case law in law school, but you might not have learned how to use them together to solve a particular legal problem.

When attacking a legal research problem, start with the applicable statute (unless the question is purely one of common law). Statutes are written broadly, so you will not likely find the ultimate answer to a research problem in a statute. The statute will give you an overview of the legal neighborhood in which an answer might be found, though. Unless the answer is already obvious, you should check to see if the statute is actually applicable to the client's situation. For this you will look first at the definitions section of the statute. Many statutes require that an entity have a minimum amount of revenue, engage in a minimum number of transactions, or have a minimum number of employees to be covered. The definitions section of the statute will also define the types of activities regulated by the statute, such as interstate commercial air transportation, or the types of entities covered, such as federally chartered banks. Sometimes, the definitions section (or another part of the statute) will state that a certain type of entity or activity is *not* covered by the statute.

You cannot believe everything you read in a statute, however. Occasionally, the definitions section of a statute will create more confusion than clarity. For example, Section 1 of the Federal Arbitration Act states that it does not apply to "contracts of employment of seamen, railroad employees, or any other class of workers engaged in foreign or interstate commerce" (9 U.S.C. § 1). On its face it would seem the Act would apply to only a very small

3. Pay attention to the red or yellow flag or symbol at the top of the first page of a case on Westlaw or Lexis. If it's a red flag or symbol, the case is probably useless because it has been reversed or overruled. If it's a yellow flag or symbol, other courts have disagreed with it. Find out why.

number of employees, since most employees are engaged in interstate or foreign commerce if they use a telephone or a computer or if they make or use a product that is shipped across state lines or is sourced from parts shipped in interstate or foreign commerce. Courts have not interpreted the statute that way, however. Statutes are creatures of a political process. Sometimes they contain language inserted to get the votes of enough legislators to pass the measure. Courts and regulators might interpret the statute differently over time, however. What a statute says is not necessarily what it means. If the meaning of a statute is unclear, you should check the legislative history of the statute to see if it shines any light. In any event, once you have determined that your client appears to be covered by the statute, you should review the statutory language to determine how the statute governs the activity that is the subject of your research question.

Regulations are promulgated by government agencies to provide more detail regarding what a statute means than the legislature was able to provide. If promulgated properly and within the authority of the agency, these regulations generally are legally binding. Always look at any applicable regulations to see if the topic of your research is addressed there. You most likely will not find the precise answer in the regulations, but they might help you narrow your focus. Again, focus on the definitions section first, to determine if the client and its activities at issue are covered by the regulations. Some regulations are very detailed. You need not read all of the regulations in detail, but you should be familiar with whether and how they apply to your client's situation.

Next, you will begin researching case law, as you should have enough background to be able to find the right section of a case digest or to construct some electronic research queries to direct you to relevant case law.[4] You will need to sort through 40 to 50 cases initially, but then you will narrow your search to between six and ten cases that are not directly on point but are somewhat

4. If you are researching a particular statute, Westlaw's Notes of Decisions or Lexis's Notes to Decisions can be a good place to start as well.

analogous. Typically, some will cut one way and some the other way. You must read each case carefully to determine which cases are closest to your situation. Often it will come down to the facts of the cases. After considering all of the cases, you should be able to say that two or three cases are close enough to your issue and your facts that you can use them to predict how a court would likely decide your issue. This is legal analysis. You will write a memo explaining your analysis of the statute, regulations, and case law and come up with an answer to the question you were assigned.

For example, assume a partner informs you that your firm represents a private country club in your city and that club received a letter from a disability rights organization demanding that the club acquire special golf carts for golfers with disabilities. The organization has threatened the club with a lawsuit under the Americans with Disabilities Act (ADA) if the club does not make the special carts available. There are two questions that need to be answered. One is whether the country club is covered by the ADA. The other is whether the ADA requires golf courses to provide special carts for disabled golfers. The partner assigns the first question to you and the second question to another associate.

The partner explains that Title III of the ADA covers "public accommodations." She explains that the client country club does not generally allow members of the public to come and play golf. It is also selective about the members it admits. No one can just show up and pay the initiation fee and be accepted. A potential member must apply and be interviewed and undergo a background investigation. She explains that the club generally limits use of its facilities to its members, but it allows local charities and nonprofits to hold fundraising golf tournaments there when nonmembers may play golf. She tells you that the club hosted a golf tournament on the professional tour last year that attracted many spectators who were charged admission to enter the club to view the tournament. The partner also informs you that the club often rents out its clubhouse to nonmembers for weddings and other celebrations, and nonmembers of the club are permitted to attend those events.

Finally, the partner informs you that on certain days, members may invite nonmembers to go golfing at the club and that several partners at the firm who are members of the club take advantage of those opportunities to invite clients to go golfing at the club. Your task, therefore, will be to determine whether the private country club is a "public accommodation" under the ADA.

You start with an overview of Title III of the ADA, which requires generally that places of public accommodation must make their facilities, goods, and services equally accessible to persons with disabilities. You examine the various sections of the ADA statute and find in it a provision stating that Title III does not apply to "private clubs" (42 U.S.C. § 12187). Some associates would stop there and declare victory. They would excitedly write a memo to the partner explaining that the country club is a private club and private clubs are not covered by the ADA, per the cited statutory language. They would think, "This legal analysis stuff is easy!" They would think the call to come to the partner's office was to receive the partner's deep gratitude and congratulations for their brilliant work.

Upon arrival at the partner's office, however, instead of congratulations they would find the partner doing her best to suppress her irritation at the associate for taking such a superficial approach to the assignment. The partner would explain that she already knows the ADA contains a section stating that private clubs are not covered, but the organization threatening to sue the club is contending that the club is not really a private club, for the reasons she explained when she gave the assignment. The partner might tell the associate to go back and look further, or she might say "never mind" and give the assignment to the associate researching the other question.

You are not like some associates, though. You know that the answer cannot be so simple because there is a potential plaintiff ready to challenge the club's status in court. You did not stop at the statute. You continued looking. You found the regulations for Title III of the ADA, and you found in the definitions section that a "private club" is defined as "a private club or establishment exempted from coverage under title II of the Civil Rights Act of 1964" (42 U.S.C. § 2000a(e)). You then looked at that statute and found that it does not apply to a "private club or other establishment not in fact open to the public, except to the extent that the facilities of such establishment are made available to the customers or patrons of" a public accommodation such as a restaurant or a place of entertainment. Although this language is far from clear, it gives you enough to frame the issue. You conclude that a private club might still be a "public accommodation" under the ADA if its dining facilities and golf course are available for use by customers or patrons who are not members. Given the facts you know about the client, it's not immediately clear whether the club would be deemed a "private club" or a "public accommodation" under the law. To find the correct answer to this question, you will need to research the case law to see how courts have viewed similar clubs.

You run a few search queries on Westlaw or Lexis. You find a case holding that a private club is not covered by Title III of the ADA where only members and their nonpaying guests are allowed to enter and use its facilities. You find another case holding that a country club owned and operated by a for-profit company is essentially a business and easily qualifies as a public accommodation. Your client's situation is somewhere in the middle, though, so you focus on three cases with facts somewhat analogous to your facts. One case holds that a country club that is not open to nonmembers did not become a public accommodation simply because it hosted a professional golf tournament to which it admitted invited guests and the media but it did not allow members of the public to attend by paying an admission fee. You find another case holding that a country club was a public accommodation as to its clubhouse because it allowed nonmembers to book events there but not as to its golf course, which was limited to members only. You find a third case holding that a country club was a public accommodation for all purposes because it allowed its clubhouse to be booked by nonmembers and because members could invite business associates to play golf there. You conclude based on these cases that the client country club likely will be found a public accommodation under the ADA because (1) it rents its clubhouse to nonmembers for events, (2) it hosted a professional golf tournament and charged admission to members of the public, (3) it allows charities and nonprofits to use the golf course for fundraisers that nonmembers attend, and (4) it allows its members to use the golf course as a means of client entertainment where nonmembers are invited to play. You write a memo to the partner stating this conclusion and your analysis, and she stops by your office to compliment your nice work.

This is a simple example of the kinds of issues you will be assigned to research and analyze. While you will want to be efficient in your work, you must take the time to research the case law sufficiently so that you find the most relevant cases. Only when you are sure you have all of the relevant cases should you start your analysis. In the course of your analysis, as you arrive at a tentative conclusion, ask yourself how likely it would be for a court to reach the *opposite* conclusion. In the previous example, you would ask yourself whether a court is likely to find the client country club *not* to be a public accommodation despite the facts that it allows nonmembers to use its facilities in so many instances and that it sometimes earns revenue from allowing nonmembers to access the club. It would not seem probable that a court would reach such a result in light of the case law, so your tentative answer is likely the correct answer.

Steering around Dead Ends

You must be careful in your research that you do not pursue dead ends that will not lead you to an acceptable answer to the question you were asked to research. Some of them are the following:

1. Authority from the wrong jurisdiction. Limit your research to the law in the jurisdiction in which the litigation is occurring or might occur. If you cannot find case authority that is even close, you can go outside of your jurisdiction, but whatever authority you might find is not binding on a court in your jurisdiction, and such a court might not even find it persuasive. Citing Fifth Circuit authority to a California state court generally will not go well, unless the Fifth Circuit case involves nearly identical facts to yours and applicable statutes that are nearly identical as well. Case law in one federal circuit will not be useful in another federal circuit where the latter circuit has its own contrary law on the subject. Federal court authority interpreting a state statute will not be controlling but might be persuasive to a state court in that state. Some state court judges, though, resist federal courts' attempts at interpreting state law. Don't think, therefore, that just because you have found a case on point in another jurisdiction, you have found the right answer. Keep pushing until you find applicable case authority in the correct jurisdiction.

2. Authority that is not binding. State trial court decisions are not binding on other trial courts in the state. Federal trial court decisions might be persuasive to other federal trial courts, but they are not binding. If you are trying to determine the law in a particular state, focus first on cases from the state's supreme court and second on intermediate appellate court decisions, especially where there is substantial case law on the issue. Only then look at decisions of federal courts in the state interpreting state law. If you can answer the question using only authority from the state supreme court, do so. If you are trying to determine federal law, focus first on cases from the federal circuit court of appeals in the relevant circuit and only then on federal district court cases in that circuit or appellate cases from other circuits.

3. Unpublished cases. Before you cite an unpublished case in a brief or research memorandum, know whether doing so is permitted in the jurisdiction involved. Some jurisdictions allow it, many do not, and a few allow it for only limited purposes. Never base your conclusion in a research memo or a key point in a brief solely on unpublished case law, moreover. If the case is unpublished, the court is not likely to give it much weight. If all you can find on point is unpublished authority, don't tell the partner, "This is all I could find." Keep looking for published cases from which you can do some legal analysis.

4. Agency "guidance." Numerous federal and state agencies issue "guidance" regarding the laws they enforce. Sometimes such guidance is meant primarily for the agency's enforcement team (but published nonetheless), and sometimes it is intended to assist the public in understanding the laws the agency enforces. Either way, it is not binding on courts. Some courts might find it persuasive; other courts might reject it outright. Only if an agency adopts a regulation through a formal rulemaking process, which involves advance notice and an opportunity for public comment, will the regulation have the force of law. This is not to say you should not review agency guidance in the course of researching an issue. It can be very helpful in understanding the legal landscape, and it might refer to case authority that you missed. You cannot base a conclusion in a research memo or a key point in a brief only on agency guidance, however, unless the question is how the agency that issued the guidance will likely decide the issue at hand.

5. Secondary sources. Secondary sources, such as *Williston on Contracts* or the *Restatements of the Law*, can be useful in gaining an understanding of an unfamiliar concept of the law. If your issue is whether a course of dealing between two parties amounted to an accord and satisfaction and you have only the foggiest memory of covering that topic in contracts class, you should refresh yourself on the topic before you dig into the case law. These secondary sources can do that for you. They cannot substitute for research into the law of the relevant jurisdiction, however. You must never rely solely on a secondary source for the answer to a question in a research memo or a key point in a brief because it reflects only the law *generally* and when the book was published some years ago, not the current law in your jurisdiction that a court will apply to your issue.

6. "Hallway research." When I was an associate, a story circulated around the firm about an associate whom one of the firm's founding partners assigned to research a particular issue. The associate could not find any law on point, so he went to the partner, a legal giant of his time, and reported that he could not find any law but "an esteemed senior associate" was of the opinion that the answer was such-and-such. Word was that the associate's career with the firm met an abrupt end that day. I thought the story might have been apocryphal, but then it happened with one of my associates. I had assigned the associate an issue to research, and he returned a couple of days later with no law that was helpful but with a survey of what some other associates thought the answer might be. It should go without saying that this will not suffice as legal research. If you simply cannot find the answer, ask the partner or a colleague or two for some tips on where to look next. It turns out there really is an answer to most legal questions. Some just take longer to find than others.

Using AI

The use of artificial intelligence (AI) in the practice of law is just getting started as of this book's writing. There are AI applications that can perform legal research and write a legal memorandum for you, but they are presently very rudimentary. That's not to say they are not useful. They can get you started on researching an issue and show you some cases you might not have found through other means. You must never submit the product of AI-driven legal research as your own work, however. That includes cutting and pasting portions of an AI-produced memo into your own work product (more on this in Chapter 4). Before you use any cases produced by AI, moreover, you must read them to ensure they say what your AI application thinks they say.

Finding the Answer Quickly

Sometimes a partner or a client will ask you a question that requires a prompt answer. You will not have a day or more to do extensive legal analysis. You must become familiar, therefore, with the resources available in your field of law to find answers quickly. They might include a treatise published by the ABA or another legal publisher or a book published by a leading practitioner in the field (but be wary of relying on a source that is not regularly updated). They might include a book containing procedural statutes and rules in your jurisdiction. They might include an enforcement manual published by the agency that enforces a particular law or a compliance guide published by an industry or trade group. You will probably come to rely on a few such resources.

Whichever resource you use, distinguish between questions that have answers that are well settled and those that have answers that are more nuanced. If the question is the length of the statute of limitations for a cause of action for conversion, the answer is likely to be well settled and you can probably find it in a manual of state statutes or a compendium of state statutes online.[5] If the question is whether an employer's failure to pay all commissions due constitutes the tort of conversion, the answer is likely to be less clear. You will probably not find the answer in a treatise or agency enforcement manual. You will need to conduct some research. If so, notify the partner or the client that finding the answer will require some brief research. Neither is likely to tell you, "No, I would rather you just wing it." Be as efficient as you can, but take the time you need to find the correct answer.

Obtaining Information from the Client

As an associate you might be assigned to respond to a demand letter or a government agency complaint or to answer opposing counsel's discovery requests in a lawsuit. Each of these tasks will require that you obtain documents and information from the

5. If you do "Google research" to find what appears to be the answer, always confirm that answer with the actual statutory language. Material published online that provides answers to these questions sometimes turns out to be incorrect or outdated.

client. There are some considerations you will want to keep in mind as you do so.

1. **Don't assume that your client did nothing wrong.** Sometimes associates assume that their client could not possibly be guilty of the violations of law alleged by a potential litigant or a government agency. This is an irrational assumption because no law firm is fortunate enough to represent only the unjustly accused. In the real world, clients screw up. If your client did, you need to know about it so that you and your supervising partner can determine how to deal with it in the context of the case. "Confirmation bias" refers to the tendency of people to look only for information that confirms their preexisting view of a subject. If at the outset of a case you believe your client did not commit the wrongdoing alleged, confirmation bias might cause you to look only for evidence that supports your belief. This does not amount to a sufficient factual investigation, however. As you conduct your investigation, therefore, do not take at face value everything you are told. Your client's employees might not readily admit that they made an error. It might take some gentle probing on your part to get to the truth, but you will need the truth in order to defend your client properly against the claims or charges presented.

2. **Be clear that you are authorized to contact the client's employees directly.** There are two aspects to this. One, be sure your supervising partner is OK with your contacting the client directly. Assuming so, you should copy the partner on all of your communications with the client. Two, be sure your client's representative is OK with your contacting that company's employees directly. She will probably ask to be copied on your communications. Copy her as well. You should ask her, moreover, for an introduction to the person(s) you will need to contact, so they know they are permitted to speak with you. Most corporate employees will not be very forthcoming when an unfamiliar lawyer calls and starts asking questions. If they are told by in-house counsel or a member of management that it's OK for them to speak with you, they are more likely to give you the information you need.

3. Recognize that client personnel whom you contact are busy. Though there will be exceptions, most of the corporate clients you will represent will be staffed leanly. The client's employees whose assistance you will need are probably going to be very busy with their own work, so recognize that your request for their assistance will be an imposition. This requires that you give them enough advance notice of your request (*never* on the day before the brief or response letter is due) and that you not come on too strongly with them. If you seem too officious or demanding, they are less likely to want to help you. This requires some finesse on your part. You must communicate the importance of your requests for information while being sensitive to the fact that they already are busy and must find time to help you.

4. Be prepared with a list of what you need before you contact the client's employees. Make a list of all of the documents you will need from each person you will contact in the client organization. Be sure your list is complete before you make any contact. Then, before you ask the client for the information, check to see if the firm already has the information in the case file. Clients do not like providing the same information multiple times to their lawyers. Once you are sure the client has not provided the information you seek, go ahead and ask for it. After each of your conversations with the client's employees requesting information, send them an email confirming the list of the documents you need. This list will help ensure that nothing is left out. Give each person a deadline for sending the items you request, but make sure you will still have enough time if the deadline you provide is not met.

5. Be prepared not to get everything you asked for. Do not be surprised if you do not get all of the items you requested. Some of the documents might not be easily accessible, or the employee of whom you made the request might not have the time to conduct a search. You might have to follow up with another polite request or two. This is why you must request documents from the client as soon as you know what you will need. It always takes much longer than you anticipated to get the items you requested.

6. Be aware that the client's employee might have the documents you need but might not want to give them to you. The documents you requested might put the employee, her boss, or the company in a bad light. They might reveal that a mistake occurred, and the employee of whom you made the request might be afraid of being fired. If the employee tells you that records cannot be found that you are fairly certain must exist, this could be the reason. If you suspect that a client is choosing not to provide documents you have requested, alert the partner right away. The partner will need to decide whether to press further for the documents and how best to do so.

Interviewing Witnesses

As part of your investigation of a case, you might be required to interview current or former employees of the client. The same advice applies as with respect to requesting documents from client employees, but even more so. You will find that most employees of a client are not eager to be interviewed by a lawyer. Even if they had no role in any wrongdoing, they still might be reluctant to get involved. They are concerned that if they say the wrong thing, they might get into trouble, or someone might lose their job. It is essential, therefore, that someone in the client's organization introduce you to the witness in advance or at the beginning of the interview.

If you are not able to do the witness interviews in person, at least try to do them by videoconference. You can evaluate a witness's credibility much more readily by observing them as they speak. A witness who seems physically uncomfortable talking with you and who does not look you in the eye could just be extremely nervous, or he might be trying to avoid revealing unfavorable information. You cannot read a witness as well in a telephone interview.

At the beginning of the interview, you must advise the witness that you are an attorney for the company. Ask them if they understand this and record their answer in your notes. This is important in order to avoid giving the witness the impression that you are their lawyer. Similarly, you must avoid providing a witness legal advice. For example, a witness might ask you if they should bring their own complaint about wrongdoing they observed or if they did the right thing in raising a complaint with management. You must reiterate that you are not their lawyer and cannot give them advice. On occasion, a witness will keep trying to adopt you as their attorney. It might simply be that they are unfamiliar with the process of being interviewed by an attorney and they are looking for guidance, or it might be that they are attempting to co-opt you to create a conflict of interest that could prevent your firm from continuing to represent the company. Either way, you need to be on your guard and continue to remind the witness that you are not their attorney and cannot advise them.

If the witness gave a written statement in the course of the client's internal investigation of the matter, have a copy of the statement handy, but do not give it to the witness right away. Rather, see if the facts the witness gives to you are consistent with the witness's written statement. If they are not, remind the witness of the written statement they provided previously and inquire about the reason for their giving a different account now. Minor variances are to be expected, but a significant difference should cause you to question the witness's credibility.

Start your interview of the witness with several background questions that will help put them at ease. Ask how long they have worked for the company. Ask which positions they have held at the company. If they have not worked for the company for very long, ask about their prior jobs. Ask them about their duties and responsibilities in their current position. If the claim you are investigating involves an alleged hostile working environment, ask some general questions about the working environment, such as how employees get along with each other, whether the manager or coworkers use profanity or disparaging language when speaking with one another, and if the manager is accessible and visible around the department.

If you are questioning the witness about a specific incident such as an industrial accident, ask them questions to set the stage for what they observed—Where were they located when the accident occurred? If it was not their usual workstation, why were they there? Was anyone else in the vicinity? Did they have a conversation with anyone just prior to the accident? How far away from the accident were they when it occurred?

Next, take the witness through what they observed in detail, step by step. Ask what they saw, what they heard, and in what order. Ask if they heard any person say anything during or just after the accident. If someone was injured in the accident, ask the witness what they observed about the injured person. Was the person unconscious? Visibly injured? Did the person walk away from the accident? Did they appear to be limping or in pain? Did they say that they were OK? Ask what physical damage occurred as a result of the accident. Was the building, equipment, or product damaged? Ask if they heard anyone, especially a member of management, say anything after the accident. Ask if they took any photos with their phone.

If the subject of your investigation is not a specific incident but something more general, such as an alleged "toxic workplace," again obtain as much detail as you can from the witness concerning what they saw or heard. Have them describe each incident they remember—What was the date and time that it occurred? Who was present? What was said and by whom? Did anyone respond or have any reaction, such as laughing or head-shaking? Did you discuss it with anyone at the time? It is important to obtain details about every alleged incident. If all the witness can say is that "it was just a feeling I had" or "it was everything, all the time," try to jog their memory about a specific incident. If they cannot relate even one specific incident, that is significant in its own way.

Take careful notes of each witness interview. If your notes are not complete or are illegible, write a memo regarding the interview immediately upon its conclusion while it is still fresh in your mind. Use quotation marks to indicate the witness's exact words. Ask your supervising partner in advance whether you should obtain a signed statement or a sworn affidavit or declaration from the witness. If there is a possibility that the employee might be leaving the company in the near future, you might want to get a signed or sworn statement. You should not take written or sworn statements from witnesses who relate information unfavorable to the client since such statements might have to be produced to the other side in discovery. Your notes of the interview, by contrast, would ordinarily constitute attorney work product that need not be disclosed. To ensure that your notes and subsequent memo will be protected as work product, include in both your notes and your memo your observations regarding the witness's demeanor, candor, and credibility.

If you do take a written statement or sworn affidavit or declaration from the witness, write it out and send it to the witness for review and signature. State in your transmittal letter or email to the witness that you did your best in drafting the statement to include everything that he or she said, but if you left anything out or recorded anything inaccurately, the witness should either edit the document accordingly or let you know what should be changed so you can provide a corrected document. It is essential that the witness be entirely comfortable with the contents of a written statement before signing it. You don't want to be accused of "putting words in the witness's mouth." Even if every word in the written statement does not support the client's position, if on balance it is more favorable than not, it's worth having. If the witness makes major changes to the draft statement so that it diverges significantly from your oral interview with the witness, raising a substantial question regarding the witness's credibility, simply tell the witness you have decided that a signed statement is not necessary.

Responding to Discovery

A substantial portion of your work as an associate will likely involve drafting responses to opposing counsel's requests for discovery—interrogatories, requests for admissions, and requests for production of documents. In addition, in federal court and in some state courts, parties are required to produce initial disclosures of relevant documents and the names and addresses of witnesses at the outset of the case. You might be called upon to manage this initial disclosure process as well.

As a new associate, you might think all of this is just paperwork—tasks to be completed by the assigned deadline. Discovery is much more than that, however. What a party produces in discovery can mean the difference between victory and defeat in a case. Many lawyers do not grasp the importance of discovery until they have tried a case or two. Since so few civil cases make it to trial these days, many new associates are unaware of how the responses they submit to their opponent's discovery requests can make or break a case. There are three key things you should remember about discovery.

1. **If you could have produced it in discovery but didn't, you probably won't be able to use it at trial.** Except for impeachment evidence that you would use to attack the credibility of a witness, most courts will not allow you to use documents at trial that were not disclosed in discovery. *The judge will not be interested at that point in hearing that the document was not produced because opposing counsel's requests were overbroad or because the document arguably was covered by some privilege.* If your side didn't produce it, you can't use it. You should not simply raise every possible objection to every discovery request, therefore. Rather, you should confer with the partner who will likely serve as lead trial counsel on the case and think together strategically about which documents and other items you will need to present at trial in order to win your case. Then you must be sure to produce those documents and other items even though your opponent's requests might be objectionable.

Be careful about the assertion of privileges, too. You never want to waive a privilege inadvertently, but you might want to waive it strategically. Let's say your client is being sued for sexual harassment from a senior executive. When the internal complaint came in, your client hired an outside law firm to investigate the claim and report back to the board of directors. The law firm's investigation found no violation of company policy and no unlawful conduct. The law firm's written report has "ATTORNEY-CLIENT PRIVILEGED COMMUNICATION" at the top of every page. Most associates would object to producing the report because, well, it's attorney-client privileged. But you are smarter than that. You know that the fact that your client conducted an impartial investigation that found no wrongdoing will be extremely helpful evidence at trial and that the partner who tries the case will likely want to call the investigator as a witness. If you refuse to produce her report, however, the court is not likely to allow her to testify. You must discuss this issue with the supervising partner because any waiver of the attorney-client privilege requires knowing and informed consent by the client, but the client likely will agree that a limited waiver of the privilege is warranted under these circumstances.

Before you start to draft discovery responses, therefore, know the theory of your case. Have a discussion with the lead trial partner about how the case will be presented at trial if it gets that far. Anticipate what documents you will need to prove your client's claims or defenses. Produce those documents even though the requests for them are objectionable.

2. If you do not produce enough evidence in discovery to support your case, you could lose a motion for summary judgment or lose at trial. You must not only produce all of the documents needed for your side to prevail at trial, but you also must provide sufficient responses to interrogatories. If you fail to do so, your opponent might move for summary judgment, and that motion could be granted. Sometimes lawyers seek to provide as little information as they can in discovery responses so as not to "give away our case." The whole point of discovery, however, is to provide fair notice to your opponent regarding the evidence and theories you plan to present at trial. The era of "trial by ambush" has long since passed.

Suppose your client is suing a service provider for breach of contract for providing documents containing errors that resulted in your client being sued by third parties. Under the contract the defendant is liable for gross negligence, intentional misconduct, or fraud but not for ordinary negligence. Your opponent sends interrogatories that ask how the services provided amounted to (1) gross negligence, (2) intentional misconduct, or (3) fraud. You respond only that the defendant produced documents containing errors that caused third parties to sue your client. Your opponent moves for summary judgment on the ground that you have not shown evidence of gross negligence, intentional misconduct, or fraud. The court might well grant such a motion, and your client would lose the case. You cannot provide superficial or evasive answers to interrogatories, therefore. To the contrary, you must know the elements of the case your side will have to prove at trial and present evidence in support of those elements in your discovery responses. In the previous case, you must show more than merely that errors were made. If it is too early in the case for you to provide a complete response, say so. State that your client has not yet had a sufficient opportunity to conduct discovery and reserves the right to supplement the response after additional discovery has been done. Then supplement your prior response if discovery reveals that other customers of the defendant put it on notice previously of similar errors that the defendant never corrected, which evidence might support a finding of gross negligence.

Providing an insufficient answer to interrogatories will not just expose your client to potential summary judgment. If the case should get to trial, your insufficient interrogatory responses might be used to impeach the credibility of your client representative who testifies at trial. Assume your client fired an employee shortly after he raised a safety complaint. The former employee sued for retaliation. The client was vague about the reasons for the employee's termination when you were collecting information for responding to interrogatories. All they gave you was that the plaintiff had an uncooperative attitude and attendance problems.

The client was very busy, and you did not push further even though you believed the client's reasons for terminating the employee were weak. Nonetheless, those were the reasons you put in the interrogatory responses. At trial, the former employee's supervisor testifies that the plaintiff was terminated for leaving work early but indicating on his time record that he worked a full day. Opposing counsel attacks the supervisor's credibility by pointing to the absence of this reason for the plaintiff's termination in your interrogatory responses, suggesting that this supposed reason for the plaintiff's termination was made up after the fact. The jury finds for the plaintiff because your client could not present a strong and consistent legitimate reason for terminating the plaintiff after he complained about safety. Therefore, should the client give you a weak or vague explanation for why they did something that is in issue in a lawsuit, keep pushing to ensure you have the complete story before answering interrogatories. There is probably a better explanation for what happened. You need to find that explanation and include it in your interrogatory responses before your client signs them under oath.

3. Playing hardball during discovery can get expensive. Some partners, and some clients, prefer to play hardball when it comes to discovery. They might want you to object to all of opposing counsel's discovery responses and make them work to get even the most basic information. What typically happens next is the exchange of lengthy "meet and confer" letters followed by motions to compel further discovery, motions for protective orders, or both. In addition to running the risk of not being able to use key evidence at trial, as illustrated earlier, all of this activity substantially increases the cost of prosecuting or defending a lawsuit. If the client is on board and is willing to pay the extra cost, fine, assuming the positions you are taking are not frivolous, but sometimes clients do not appreciate the expense of such a strategy until they receive your firm's first few invoices. If you have a client that insists on fighting every attempt by the other side to obtain discovery, alert your supervising partner so that a discussion may be had with the client, if need be, about the wisdom and cost of such an approach.

Obtaining Feedback about Your Work

You will want to obtain partner feedback regarding the quality of your work to the extent you can. Asking a partner for feedback regarding every assignment is too much, however. You will likely annoy partners to the point they will not want to work with you. Also, while sometimes a partner will go to the trouble of redlining changes to your draft and adding comments in the margin, you cannot expect all partners to critique your work like your college professors did. Partners are simply too busy. If the partner did not send you a redlined edit of your draft, compare what you submitted to the final document that was filed or served, and you should be able to spot the key changes. If the partner made many substantial changes to your draft and you are unclear as to why, ask him, but wait until after the rush to get the document filed or served has passed.

You should find time to ask the partner for some feedback regarding your contributions at the conclusion of a major project or case. In most instances partners will give you a balanced and meaningful critique. Listen especially to the less than flattering parts of the critique and learn from them. Don't be defensive. Express your thanks to the partner for taking time to give you feedback, then make notes. In fact, you might consider keeping folders on your computer desktop for each partner with whom you work. Store in those folders notes about the partner's working style, any special requirements or expectations the partner communicated to you regarding working with him or her, and all of the feedback you received from the partner about your work. All of this information will help you work more effectively with the partner in the future.

Your firm will probably provide you with some sort of annual performance evaluation. In larger firms the evaluating attorneys' feedback might not be reported verbatim and with attribution but rather might be blended with the feedback from others so that you will not be able to identify a specific evaluator. If your evaluation is ambiguous or difficult to interpret, ask your mentor, your office managing partner, or a member of the evaluation committee (if there is one) for an explanation. Firms also sometimes send signals to associates regarding their performance in the form of pay raises. If other associates received pay raises but you did not, you should worry. If you received a larger pay raise than other associates in your class, you should read from it that the firm is pleased with your performance.

Another accurate form of feedback about your work performance you will receive is your continued workload. In Chapter 10 we will address the internal and external marketplaces in which a lawyer operates. How busy you remain over time is probably the best measure of how you are doing. This is because if partners like your work, they will want to continue working with you. This is the internal marketplace at work. If the marketplace values your performance, it will give you more work. If the firm is busy and your workload is slow, however, you should discuss the situation with your mentor and perhaps solicit some feedback from partners with whom you recently worked. You must do your best to learn what is holding partners back from assigning you new work. It might not be the quality of your work. It might be your work habits. Perhaps you missed a deadline, or you work remotely more than the firm prefers. Whatever you have done to make partners reluctant to work with you again, fix it. Ask partners for another chance to work with them, and if they give it to you, be sure to show them that you have corrected the problems.

Getting Your Firm Paid for Your Work

While as a junior associate you will not be responsible for billing firm clients (unless you generate clients of your own), you will have an important role in the billing process nonetheless. This is because every time entry that you write, unless edited or written off, will be seen by the client. This is your opportunity to communicate the value of your legal work to the client. It is also in your own interest that your time entries are billed to and paid by the client. Most firms keep track of not only the number of hours billed by each lawyer but also the revenue generated by that lawyer's time billed. If you bill 2,200 hours but the firm is able to collect payment for only 1,500 of them, you will not be as valuable to the firm as a lawyer who bills 1,800 hours and the firm is able to collect payment for 1,750 of them.

Another reason you will want to take care to write accurate billing entries is that most firms generate draft invoices by computer and the billing partner must review and edit the invoices before they are sent. Partners typically review and edit their draft bills late at night and on weekends. If you submit time entries that are garbled or incoherent, the partner will probably not chase you down to find out what you were trying to say. She likely will simply write off that entry from the invoice, and you will lose credit for the time you billed.

When you write your time entries, think "Goldilocks." Not too little, not too much. Just right. For example, clients will not accept an entry for eight hours of time that says only "8.0 Research" or "8.0 Drafted brief." Nor will a client want to see something like this:

0.2 Strategized regarding brief.

0.2 Reviewed notes for drafting brief.

0.4 Reviewed cases for brief.

0.5 Drafted outline for brief.

1.0 Drafted introduction for brief.

2.2 Drafted statement of facts for brief.

0.2 Checked statute to confirm statute of limitations.

0.8 Drafted argument that plaintiff's claim fell outside statute of limitations.

0.5 Drafted argument that plaintiff failed to exhaust internal remedies.

1.0 Drafted argument that plaintiff's complaint fails to state a claim.

0.5 Drafted conclusion.

0.5 Further review of case authority to ensure all available arguments were presented.

That's too much detail. This is better:

1.0 Reviewed and organized case law and outlined arguments for brief.

1.0 Drafted introduction for brief.

2.0 Drafted statement of facts for brief.

4.0 Drafted legal argument section of brief.

There are some time entries on invoices that really irritate billing partners (and their clients). They include:

1. "Reviewed executed settlement agreement. 0.2" Just what were you reviewing exactly? Whether the signatures appeared to be authentic? The agreement was signed by DocuSign! This is that last grasp for billing credit before closing the file. Partners hate it and clients are offended by it. Don't do it.

2. "Prepared for oral argument. 1.0" This might be OK if you presented the argument (although I would probably add a bit more detail). But you did not present the argument! I did! How did your preparation for my oral argument (that you never shared with me, by the way) add value to the case?

3. "Discussed new assignment with partner. 0.4" You cannot bill a client for accepting a new work assignment. Most clients (and especially insurance companies) will not pay for interoffice conferences that do not demonstrably add value. "Discussion with partner regarding arguments to include in motion for summary judgment" will probably pass muster. "Discussion with partner about case" will not.

4. "Brainstormed about case with other associates. 0.5" You cannot bill for talking with your colleagues about your case.

5. "Explained to assistant that brief must be filed electronically with the court with a courtesy copy to chambers. 0.2" You cannot bill for speaking to your legal assistant.

6. "Left message for opposing counsel. 0.2" You cannot bill for simply leaving a message for someone.

7. "Email to J. Jones re scheduling interview. 0.2" You cannot bill for simply scheduling an interview. It would be different if you accomplished something more than simply scheduling: "Emailed J. Jones re scheduling witness interview along with list of topics to be covered and documents needed."

8. "Reviewed local rules. 1.0" You cannot bill for simply reviewing the local court rules in your home jurisdiction. You are expected to know them. If your case is in an unfamiliar jurisdiction and your review is of a specific portion of the rules relevant to your current work, an entry such as the following will likely be accepted: "Reviewed key provisions of Napa County local rules for compliance with initial case requirements."

9. "Organized exhibits. 0.5" This sounds like clerical work, which clients will not pay for. If what you were doing was going through the file to select appropriate exhibits for the brief, say so. "Reviewed incident file and selected exhibits for response to agency complaint" is attorney work that clients typically will not question.

The list could go on. When in doubt, ask yourself: "If I were the client, would I pay for that?" You cannot bill clients for every waking moment you are at work. If it does not add value, don't bill for it.

There is more you can do to make the billing partner's life easier:

1. Be sure your client and matter codes are correct. If your time erroneously winds up on the draft bill of a partner in another office, it almost certainly will be written off. Even if the time is on the right client but the wrong matter, it takes billing attorney and staff time to move the entry to the correct matter.

2. Be consistent in your reference to names. Don't keep switching from "Mr. Smith" to "John Smith" to "J. Smith." For client representatives and corporate witnesses, I prefer first initial and last name: "Witness interview of J. Smith." If your firm has a different preference, follow it. Do not refer to your client in time entries as "Plaintiff" or "Defendant." You may refer to the opposing party as "Plaintiff" if there is only one plaintiff. If there are more than one, say "Plaintiff Jones." Refer to your opposing counsel as "opposing counsel," as the client might not know that her name is Susan Brown. Refer to the court as "the court," not "the Court" and not "Judge Clark."

3. Spell your client's name correctly! It is embarrassing for a law firm to send a bill to a client with the client representative's name misspelled. Be sure you correctly spell the names of the client's employees with whom you deal, and pay special attention to those with uncommon names.

4. Follow your firm's conventions for describing meetings and telephone calls. If your firm has standard descriptions of telephone calls (telephone conference with __________ re ______________) or meetings (meeting with ___________ re ________________), use them. If your firm does not have a preference, be consistent in your descriptions. Don't switch randomly among "phone conference," "telephone conference," "telephone call," and so on. Likewise, do not variably use "meeting," "conference," and "discussion," for example.

5. Do not reveal sensitive information in your billing entries. Several people in the client organization will likely see your firm's invoice as it moves from the legal department to the accounting department for payment, with a possible stop at the business unit leader's office. Do not put information in your billing entries such as "telephone conference with S. King re company-wide layoff" or "meeting with P. Jensen re termination of senior vice president of operations." Be discreet. The same goes for settlement demands and offers. Do not put "emails with S. King re settlement offer of $175,000 to Plaintiff" in a time entry, as gossip might soon start to spread in the client's organization about the terminated employee who sued and got $175,000. A simple "emails with S. King re settlement offer" will be just fine.

6. If the client or insurance carrier has special billing guidelines, obtain them, read them, and follow them. Many larger corporate clients and insurance companies issue billing guidelines for outside counsel. For example, many clients and almost all insurance companies prohibit "block billing" where you write a single narrative of all of the work you performed on a particular case in a given day. Rather, they require that each task, and the time taken to perform it, be listed separately. If the case you are working on is subject to client or insurance carrier billing guidelines, be sure to follow them when writing your time entries. If you do not, the client or insurance company might refuse to pay for the nonconforming billing entries. Sometimes the problem can be fixed by submitting a new invoice, but that takes up substantial time of both your firm's billing staff and the billing partner. That wasted time can be avoided by following the guidelines.

4

Your Written Work Product

The primary means by which lawyers communicate is by writing. You must master the basics of good legal writing to succeed as a lawyer. You can have a brilliant legal mind, but it will go unnoticed unless you can communicate effectively in writing. This is often a challenge for lawyers. Nonetheless, it is essential that you develop excellent writing skills as a junior lawyer because poor writing skills will hold you back in your professional development. You probably learned in law school how to write a research memo and a rudimentary appellate brief. That's a start, but there is much more to learning how to write effectively as a lawyer.

Many excellent books have been written on how to write effectively as a lawyer, and you should pick one or two and read them. In this chapter we will not go over everything covered in those books. Rather, we will focus on some of the key aspects of legal writing that are especially important for you to master as a part of your career advancement.

Write for Your Audience

One problem that some lawyers have is that they only have one approach to legal writing that they try to use for various different applications—briefs, research memos, letters to clients, letters to opposing counsel. It's typically part analysis and part advocacy, but it is not a particularly effective specimen of either. One size, as they say, does not fit all.

Rather, you must write differently depending upon who will be reading it. As a junior lawyer, most of your writing will fall into two principal and distinct categories: analysis and advocacy. When you are writing a research memo, you are presenting analysis. You are giving the answer to the question you were assigned to research. Maybe the law is in your client's favor, maybe not. You must be objective. Sometimes junior lawyers are afraid to present a conclusion that is at odds with what they think the partner or the client expects, and they shade their writing to avoid presenting an unfavorable conclusion directly, or they dance around the question and never really get to a clear answer. This is a mistake. If you are reasonably certain that the client will violate the law by pursuing its proposed course of conduct, and you have substantial legal authority to back you up, say so. Don't use hedging language such as "It could be argued that the client will be in violation of the law." It's better for the partner (and the client) to know now that the law is not favorable than to have them discover it after they have traveled some distance down the wrong road.

The same rationale applies to your written communications directly to a client. A partner might ask you to draft a letter to a client analyzing the client's potential liability under various legal theories, or a client might ask you a particular legal question and ask you to send them a written response. You must give the client a clear and correct answer even though it's not what they are hoping to hear. In this context you are not advocating, you are providing analysis that will guide the client's actions. Preventing your client from making an error that will lead to liability is one of the most valuable services a lawyer can perform.

Initially you will probably write research memos for partners or other senior lawyers in your firm. Determine how much formality your reader expects. Perhaps your reader wants a memo with the same formal structure as you learned in law school: (1) introduction, (2) statement of facts, (3) issue(s) presented, (4) analysis (broken down by headings and subheadings), and (5) conclusion. You might be expected to follow this format if you are drafting a memo for a client's board of directors or executive team. Where internal research memos are concerned, a partner is less likely to care as much about the formality of your structure as the substance of your analysis, and perhaps a simple email will be preferred to a formal memo. Things move much more rapidly in a law firm than in law school, and it's important now that you are a lawyer to get to the point quickly. When you receive a research assignment, ask the lawyer giving you the assignment what format they would prefer for your response.

Whether you are writing a research memo or an advice letter or email to a client, cite to the legal authority that is directly on point, whether it's a statute, a regulation, or precedential case law. As illustrated in the last chapter, however, often there will not be legal authority directly on point, and you must analyze how a court or government agency is likely to decide your case in light of the law that currently exists. Limit your discussion to that law, however. There is no need to start with a discussion of broad principles of law or decades-old U.S. Supreme Court cases. If the issue is whether the client will be liable for sexual harassment by a coworker where the victim of the harassment did not report it before she quit, there is case law in almost every federal circuit and in many states on this question. Move directly to discussing the case law in the relevant jurisdiction. Do not begin with a recitation that Congress outlawed sex discrimination in Title VII of the Civil Rights Act of 1964, and in *Meritor Savings Bank v. Vinson* in 1986, the U.S. Supreme Court held that sexual harassment can be a form of sex discrimination. You *might* start an appellate brief in this fashion (although I think there are better ways to start appellate briefs). It wastes time and space in a research memo or client communication, however. By now everyone knows that sexual harassment is generally unlawful.

If you are writing a brief to a court or government agency or a response to a demand letter, by contrast, you will be engaged in advocacy. You will not be presenting an objective analysis; you will be advocating for your client's position. For example, you will argue that your client is not liable for the accident or that the court should compel the dispute to binding arbitration. You will not want to ignore adverse legal authority, but instead of addressing it objectively, you will argue why it does not apply to the specific facts in your case.

The level of formality in your writing of advocacy will vary depending on your audience. Writing a brief for the U.S. Supreme Court or your state's supreme court, or for federal or state courts of appeals, requires a high level of formality. Those courts have rules that specify in detail what must be included in a brief and in which order. Writing a brief for a trial court requires less formality, as those courts have many cases on their calendar and need to focus on the key issues quickly. Writing a brief to a government agency or an arbitrator or mediator often warrants less formality too. Writing to opposing counsel should be even less formal. By less formal, I do not mean don't worry about spelling and grammar, or it's OK to use slang and snark.[6] What I mean is that a brief to a trial court may be structured less formally than an appellate brief (there is generally no need to include an "issues presented" section, for example, and you should only include essential facts). Less formal advocacy, such as briefs to mediators or responses to government agency investigators, may be presented in the form of a letter as opposed to in a pleading format.

Contract Writing Is Not Just a Different Animal, It's a Whole Different Zoo

Most of you will also write contracts and agreements at some point during your legal career. Settlement agreements are a fairly simple type of contract. Executive employment contracts

6. Yes, "snark" is a word. Ask Merriam-Webster.

and stock option agreements can be a bit more complex. Commercial leases and corporate acquisition or finance agreements can be among the most complex you will encounter. If you are writing these agreements, you will want to follow the appropriate contract writing style, *but do not use contract writing style for other types of legal writing!* It is essential that you recognize that contract writing is a distinct type of writing from analysis or advocacy. An essential element of contract writing is precision. Courts look at contracts to determine what the parties intended, so every word, every phrase has meaning. As a result, to ensure clarity, lawyers who draft contracts usually include many defined terms. A defined term usually appears initially capitalized and in quotes and sometimes is in parentheses; for example, ("Defined Term").

Defined terms are important for distinguishing among various parties and among other persons, entities, dates, and subjects that are addressed in an agreement. For example, you might write a settlement agreement starting as follows:

> This Settlement Agreement ("Agreement") is entered into by and among Plaintiffs John Doe ("Doe"), Mary Roe ("Roe"), and Thomas Toe ("Toe") (collectively "Plaintiffs"), and Defendants Frank Flow ("Flow"), Gregory Grow ("Grow"), and Sarah Slow ("Slow") (collectively "Defendants"), with Plaintiffs and Defendants collectively referred to as the "Parties," with respect to the settlement of the lawsuit entitled *John Doe, et al. v. Frank Flow, et al.*, in the Superior Court of Fulton County, Georgia (the "Court"), Case No. 22-02345-GLW (the "Action").

In writing contracts, unfortunately, it is often necessary to write tedious and prolix sentences such as the previous one in order to clearly define and differentiate the parties and the subjects of the agreement.

Sometimes junior lawyers who have had exposure to contract writing do not differentiate between writing contracts and writing analysis or advocacy, and they write something like this:

> On July 16, 2023 (the "Subject Date"), Lily Larson ("Larson"), an employee of Big Corporation ("BC" or "Client"), entered

> the Nashville facility of BC (the "Premises") using her employee badge, and she proceeded to the unoccupied security office ("Security Office") where she disabled the security cameras monitoring the corridor of said Premises leading to the laboratory ("Laboratory"). She then proceeded to said Laboratory. Thereafter, she was found by a security officer ("Officer") as she attempted to open the door to said Laboratory with what appeared to the Officer to be burglar tools. Larson was detained by the Officer until the Nashville Police Department ("NPD" or the "Police") arrived and arrested her.

Geez! Your reader will be exhausted upon finishing your first paragraph. Unlike in contract writing, you must use defined terms sparingly when writing analysis or advocacy. "Sparingly" means only where absolutely necessary. Most of the defined terms in the previous paragraph are not only unnecessary, but they also clutter the narrative, making it difficult to follow. This reads much better:

> In the predawn hours of Sunday, July 16, 2023, Big Corporation ("Company") employee Lily Larson used her employee badge to enter the Nashville location of the Company. She went to the unoccupied security office where she disabled the security cameras monitoring the hallway leading to the laboratory. She then walked down that hallway to the laboratory. Shortly afterward, a security guard caught her trying to open the laboratory door with burglar tools. He held Larson and called the police, who came and arrested her.

Another remnant of contract writing that sometimes finds its way into analysis or advocacy is writing numbers twice: "The truck failed four (4) inspections before the accident." While a number might be written this way in a contract just to be sure everyone understands that the parties really mean FOUR, it only clutters other forms of legal writing.

If you ever catch yourself using contract writing techniques when writing analysis or advocacy, *stop*! Put the contract language away and go back to normal legal writing.

"Draft" Is a Widely Misunderstood Term

Many new lawyers make a fundamental error at the start of their careers because they misunderstand the meaning of the term "draft." You might think of a draft as a document in rough form, to be reviewed and edited substantially before it becomes final. That's not what it means in a law firm or to your client, however. To the partners in your firm and the firm's clients, a "draft" means a document that is essentially *perfect*, except that the partner or the client might want to make a small change or a fact correction in a couple of places. You simply must not give a document to a partner or a client that is still in need of substantial revision or supplementation or that still has spelling or grammatical errors that must be corrected. It is your job to take care of all of those things before you present the document to the partner or the client.

This means that you must give yourself plenty of time to get the document into pristine shape. Give yourself time to produce several successive versions of the document if necessary. If you need more facts or information to complete the document, get them from the partner or the client before you finish writing. Do not leave blanks in the document for the partner or client to fill in, and do not leave comments in the margins or notes in brackets saying such things as "[need full names of witnesses]" or "[need to verify dates]." If you are writing a brief and you are not sure whether to include a particular argument, discuss it with the partner before you complete your draft. Be sure your draft conforms to any applicable page limits, too. We'll cover proofreading in more detail later in this chapter, but you must make certain that every "draft" you submit is thoroughly proofread before you submit it.

Always Start with an Outline

Once you have gathered all of the facts you need and have completed your research of the applicable law, don't start writing the brief, memo, or letter just yet. Write an outline first instead. The outline will give you an overview of what the final written product will say. It is important that you know where you are going before you start writing. I can always tell when I am reading a document that was not preceded by an outline. The document seems poorly organized and does not flow. You do not want your reader thinking that they are following your argument only to have it veer off in an unexpected direction.

Your outline should be the road map for the orderly progression of your argument. Suppose you are writing a brief in opposition to a motion to dismiss your client's lawsuit against a former employee for misappropriating trade secrets and using them to divert your client's customers to his new employer. The motion to dismiss argues that the information the former employee took did not amount to trade secrets and that the former employee committed no legal wrong in contacting the customers he served when he worked for your client. Your outline of your argument might look like this:

1. The defendant ex-employee took not only the customers' names but also their contact information (including cell phone numbers and email addresses), their order history, and their pricing structure.

2. The foregoing information has economic value from not being generally known by others, and your client took reasonable efforts to keep the information secret.

3. The information taken also constitutes "confidential information" covered by the confidentiality and nondisclosure agreement signed by the defendant upon being hired by your client.

4. The defendant used the information taken not merely to notify the customers that he moved to a new company but to solicit them to do business with his new company by offering them better pricing than your client offered.

5. Seven customers terminated their business relationships with your client and moved their business to the defendant's new employer, causing a loss of more than $300,000 in business for your client.

6. The defendant's conduct amounts to
(a) a violation of the Uniform Trade Secrets Act;
(b) a breach of the defendant's confidentiality and nondisclosure agreement; and
(c) tortious interference with contract and/or prospective business advantage.

If you take the time to write such an outline, it will be easier to start writing, and your writing will flow easily from one point to the next. Yes, I know you are impatient to begin writing the brief because it took a lot longer than you expected to get all of the facts from the client and research the relevant case law, and now you think you must start writing immediately in order to finish the brief on time. The half hour or so you spend writing your outline, however, will be a worthwhile investment, and it will make writing the brief go much more quickly than if you start writing immediately and lurch from topic to topic without an outline.

Cover Every Base

Too frequently when I read a draft of a brief, I have the sense that something is missing, even though all of the pages are there. What is usually missing is a response to some of the case law cited by the opposing lawyer and even sometimes some of opposing counsel's arguments. Not addressing every argument and case cited by your opponent is not acceptable legal writing. Although you might not think an argument or case citation is worthy of attention, the court might disagree, and where will that leave you? That you have a page limit is not an excuse to leave out important portions of your brief. If you are out of room, you will need to go back and edit the brief so that you have more room to fit in what you left out initially.

Even if one or more of your opponent's arguments sound ridiculous to you, you still must address them in your brief. You need not spend much time on them. Simply cite a case or two on point that refute the argument and move on. You can even do so in a footnote if you are seriously short on space. You also could group all of your opponent's apparent throwaway arguments and address them together at the end of your brief under a heading of "Plaintiff's Remaining Arguments Are without Merit."

Similarly, you must address every citation of legal authority that appears in your opponent's brief. You might find that some of them are quite far afield from the relevant issues in the motion, but you must still explain to your reader why they do not apply in your case. Again, use a footnote if you must, but do not leave any citation of authority unanswered. When you think you have finished the first draft of your brief, take a hard copy of your opponent's brief and manually check off every argument and citation of authority that you addressed in your draft. If anything is left unchecked, go back and work a discussion of it into your brief.

Never Cut and Paste

I can always tell when part of a brief was cut and pasted from somewhere else—a previous brief, an article or treatise, or the product of an AI legal research tool. I can tell because the citation style is almost always different[7] and because the syntax and flow of the writing suddenly change. If I can detect cutting and pasting so readily, I have to assume that other partners and most judges can detect it as well.

Not only does cutting and pasting make you seem like a lazy lawyer and undermine your credibility, but it is also dangerous. You don't know if what you are cutting and pasting is actually correct. You don't know if the author of what you are using even read the cases and applied them properly to the argument presented. You could be citing authority that is wildly off base. Another big problem with simply cutting and pasting language from a case from sources other than the case itself is that while the language from the case might be correctly transcribed, the holding in the case may be directly opposite of your position in your case. If you

7. For example, the words "Superior Court" appear in different citations in the same brief as "Superior Court," "Super. Ct.," and "Sup. Ct."

simply cut and paste the language from the case and add the case citation, you will not know this.

Let's say for example that you are arguing in a brief that a consumer's claim against the manufacturer of a defective product must be submitted to binding arbitration per the agreement she signed when she purchased the product, despite the fact that she now claims she did not know what she was signing. The law on this issue is fairly straightforward, so you lifted some case law and some language from one of the cases in a brief you found in your firm's brief library, but you didn't bother reading the cases you cited because you were running behind on meeting your deadline. Then, when you are standing before the court arguing your motion, your opponent says, "It's interesting that the defendant cites the *Morales* case, because in that case although the court recognized that ordinarily a consumer who signs an arbitration agreement must arbitrate and cannot claim not to have understood what she was signing, the court held that where the defendant has created arbitration agreements in other languages and did not offer such an agreement to a consumer who cannot read English, the consumer is not bound to arbitrate. My client does not speak or read English, and she requested an agreement in Spanish that we know the defendant has prepared, but they never offered it to her." At that point, you will have likely lost your motion and, worse, appeared to the court to be a careless or lazy lawyer.

Had you instead read the entire *Morales* decision before citing it in your brief, you might have chosen to cite a different case, or at least you would have been prepared to address the lack of an arbitration agreement in Spanish. Therefore, you must always read in their entirety the cases you cite in your brief.

Write Persuasively

When you are writing as an advocate, your goal is to convince your reader to see the case your way. This is the art of persuasion. You will want to persuade the court or agency that your argument produces the only lawful and equitable result. To get there you will need to show your reader why your arguments are sounder than your opponent's. Courts and government agencies read a lot of briefs, however. They approach your case with a healthy skepticism. They will not see it your way simply because you tell them that they must. Your opponent is telling them just the opposite. They will not be convinced if you simply repeat your points over and over. They will definitely not be convinced by your use of colorful adjectives to attack your opponent's position or if you yell at them in print (more on this in the next section).

Persuasive writing has three components. The first is telling a coherent and compelling story. You must present the facts of your case in an orderly fashion that communicates a convincing narrative. It might be that a chronological account is the best means of doing so, but not necessarily. If your chronology is long and generally boring, focus instead on the most important events in your case in the order of their importance. You can add a sense of their timing later. If you are writing about an accident where you allege that both the other driver and the hospital were negligent, do not spend a lot of time introducing the characters or events preceding the accident. Start with the accident:

> On August 14, 2022, Plaintiff Deborah Driver had the green light at the intersection of Route 60 and Jasper Road. Tom Trucker, distracted by a text message he received from his estranged wife, ran the red light and hit Driver broadside at a high rate of speed, flipping her SUV over three times until it landed off the road in a ravine. Driver was critically injured and was taken to Hometown Hospital. There, instead of airlifting Driver to University Medical Center, doctors who were not Board certified in neurosurgery treated her incompetently, leaving her brain-damaged and paraplegic.

You need for your opening paragraph to pack a punch, not be tangled up in irrelevant details and defined terms. You can get to those later if you must. Focus instead on telling a story that will make an impression on your reader. If you are able to tell your story in such a way that your reader becomes emotionally aligned with your side before even reading your legal argument, you are writing persuasively.

You're probably thinking, "Well, that's not possible in every piece of legal writing. Poorly answered interrogatories do not carry the same emotional impact as a terrible vehicular accident." Perhaps not, but that does not mean you cannot draw your reader in and make your subject interesting. Instead of the usual plodding narrative found in briefs addressing discovery disputes, try something like this:

> Plaintiff alleges in this case that her being fired from a job she held for only four months was so traumatic that she has been unable to bring herself to seek a new job and that she might never be able to work again. Yet, when defendant sent her interrogatories seeking detail regarding her alleged injuries and any treatment she received, she initially responded only with objections that defendant was trying to invade her privacy. When pressed for substantive responses, she answered that she does not remember the names of any of the doctors she saw or where they are located. She failed completely to answer questions regarding the number of treatment sessions she had, what diagnoses she received, and whether she was prescribed and took any medications. Defendant simply cannot defend itself against Plaintiff's serious allegations in this case without this important information.

A judge reading this paragraph will likely conclude that the plaintiff and her counsel are playing games and that a forceful response from the court is in order before ever reaching your legal authorities.

You must be careful that you do not exaggerate your facts to try to make them seem more exciting than they really are. Doing so will ruin your credibility with your reader. You do not need to exaggerate, however. There is a reason you are before the court. Your client would not spend the money for you to be there if it was not important. Communicate the importance of your issue in your presentation of your facts. If you were taught in law school that your statement of facts must be dry and boring, you were taught incorrectly. Include all of the factual detail necessary to support the arguments you will make, but tell your story in a compelling way.

The second component of persuasive legal writing involves the way you present the legal authorities supporting your position. On occasion, there might be binding precedent that compels only one result. If it is that clear, you probably would not be before the court, but in the event you are, simply tell the court that the Supreme Court's *Gunderson* case is on point and requires a ruling in your favor. There is no need for the underlining, all caps, bold, and italics that accompany many lawyers' informing the court that there is a case on point. Screeching to the judge that "as the **Supreme Court** in *Gunderson* made ***abundantly clear***, this Court **MUST** ***grant Defendant's motion!***" is not going to be any more convincing to the court than a simple statement that *Gunderson* is on point. It will only make you appear to be unhinged.

In most of your cases, though, there will not be controlling authority on point, so you will have to construct an argument using the authorities that exist that will convince the court that the result you seek fits better with existing law than the result your opponent seeks. This is the legal analysis we covered in the last chapter. The best way to do this is to make the authorities in your favor come alive. If there is a statute or regulation that strongly supports the result you seek, don't just paraphrase it, quote it verbatim. If you can do so without block quoting it, do so. If its length requires a block quote, then block quote it, but quote only the language that is relevant to your issue. Again, go easy on the italics, bold font, and the like. If there are some words that are particularly important, italicize them (and indicate that you have added the emphasis), but you don't need to italicize, bold, *and* underline them.

When you discuss cases that support your position, make the cases come alive as well. I am unimpressed when I see a lawyer make a statement of law or quote some language from a case and then merely cite the case and move on without providing any further context. That's not persuasive. Instead, discuss the key facts of the case and how they are similar to the facts in your case. Then discuss how the court reached the result it did and how the result you seek is similar to the result in the case you cite. Quote some of the court's language in the case you cite to illustrate the court's reasoning. Then do the same thing with respect to the next-strongest supporting case, and so on. You probably don't need to discuss more than three cases in this fashion to support a particular point in your argument.

Avoid long string citations. They are not persuasive, they just take up space, and they might not even say what you are representing that they say. If there are multiple cases supporting a point you are making and you do not have room for a full discussion of each, cite two of them after your presentation of the principal case and include a parenthetical for each case explaining why it supports your position.

You must also distinguish case authority that is not in support of your position. Some will tell you that if you are the moving party, let your opponent discuss the opposing authority and you can address it in your reply brief. I think it's better to play offense than to play defense, however. If you mention unfavorable authority in your opening brief and distinguish it from your case, you will bolster your credibility with the court, and you will force your opponent to play defense. You can usually distinguish unfavorable authority by showing how different the facts are in that case compared to your case. Also, look at whether courts in subsequent cases have distinguished an unfavorable case or chosen not to follow it. Even if a bad case has not been overruled, it might have fallen out of favor.

The third component of persuasive writing involves convincing the decision-maker that the result you seek is the *right* result. Unless there is controlling authority directly on point, a court will not side with you simply because you have legal authorities that support your position. The court will want to reach a just result, not simply reward the smartest lawyer with the best research skills. You must further convince the court that the result you seek is the most equitable result under the circumstances. There are a number of themes that you might invoke. With respect to discovery, it might be "Plaintiff has leveled serious charges in this case, and due process requires that the defendant gain access to plaintiff's medical records to defend itself." If you are opposing a motion to dismiss, it might be "Plaintiff should have the opportunity to conduct some discovery regarding her claims before the court takes the drastic step of dismissing her case." If there is a preliminary injunction at stake, the argument might be "This court must order the defendant to cease contacting the plaintiff's customers using the plaintiff's trade secrets, as her continuing to do so is destroying the plaintiff's business." If you are on the other side of that case, your theme might be "This court should deny the injunction because the plaintiff is trying to prevent the defendant from earning an honest living in the only profession she knows." Explain to the court why your client must prevail, apart from your argument that the legal authorities require it. In most cases if you can convince the court that you should win as a matter of the equities, the court will find a rationale in the law to rule in your favor.

Shockingly, You Shouldn't Write Like That!

Judges hate it when attorneys launch ad hominem attacks on each other in the courtroom. They equally dislike it when attorneys do so in their briefs. There is an unfortunate tendency among some lawyers toward assuming that the lawyers on the other side of the case are bad people simply because they represent the opposing party in a lawsuit. There is an even greater tendency to jump to the conclusion that opposing counsel are dishonest or unethical merely because they do not agree with you about the merits of the litigation or the propriety of certain attempts at discovery. You must resist this state of mind when writing as an advocate.

Avoid making bombastic statements such as "The plaintiff's discovery requests are shockingly overbroad." They might well be overbroad, but overbroad discovery requests are hardly "shocking." Likewise, avoid using such terms as "a joke," "laughable," or "clownish" to describe your opponent's position. Avoid characterizing your opponent's conduct or arguments with over-the-top words such as "abominable," "appalling," "despicable," "disgraceful," "dishonest," "deceitful," or "shameful." Use of such language almost always raises the temperature of a case, and it runs the risk of alienating the court.

Also, avoid words such as "tellingly" or "suspiciously" where an opponent has failed to address a point that you think should have been addressed: "Tellingly, Plaintiff fails to address the *Frostingham* case." It suggests, without proof, that your opponents were deliberately attempting to hide something from the court or that they were afraid to address the case. Maybe they never found the *Frostingham* case. By all means, point out to the court that your opponents ignored *Frostingham*, but avoid suggesting an ulterior motive.

You need not be so polite in your critique of your opponent's position that your writing is bland and your advocacy is ineffective, however. You can do better than merely stating "Plaintiff's argument lacks merit." You may attack your opponent's position and arguments with words such as "groundless," "frivolous," "devoid of merit," "dubious," "peculiar," "wrong," or even "absurd" to make your point forcefully. For example, you can say, "Plaintiff makes the absurd argument that a public entity is not entitled to invoke the attorney-client privilege." That's different, though, from suggesting that your opposing counsel is a liar, a fraud, or a terrible human being.

Write Like a Regular Person

Can you imagine going to a restaurant with friends or family and announcing to your dining companions: "If the server delivers the meal I requested, I will have no alternative but to consume it"? Or telling the neighborhood kid who walks your dog: "Please cease and desist forthwith from any further walking of my canine"? Or calling to make an appointment with your doctor and, when asked what is wrong, stating, "I have been rendered sick, sore, lame, and disabled"? People don't talk like that, and you should not write like that, either.

I am always amused when I read in a demand letter, "If your client does not pay my client the sum of $100,000 by June 1, 2024, we will be forced to file a lawsuit against your client without further notice." The lawyers never say who will "force" them to file a lawsuit. I am thinking their kidnappers already are quite lenient in allowing them to write such letters while in captivity, and so they probably won't force the lawyers to file lawsuits against their will.

Similarly, I smile when opposing counsel who does not like our discovery responses writes: "If you do not supplement your discovery responses by Friday, May 24, 2024, we will have no other option but to file a motion to compel further discovery." This is not a true statement, however. Opposing counsel has plenty of options if we do not send them discovery responses more to their liking by their unilaterally imposed deadline. Those options include picking up the phone and calling me to try to work out a compromise or simply leaving it alone and scheduling a Rule 30(b)(6) deposition to try to obtain the information another way.

Don't use this silly language when you communicate an ultimatum to your opposing counsel. Do not tell them you will take them to court if you do not mean it. If you mean it, simply tell them that if they do not provide complete responses to your discovery requests by a given date, you will file a motion to compel discovery. If they fail to do so, file your motion, but don't suggest that you are being controlled by unseen forces.

Likewise, when you write, avoid using archaic words such as "hereinabove," "hereinbelow," "hereinbefore," "hereinafter," "herewith," "therewith," "whereupon," "thereupon," and so on. If you use these words, you might as well start every piece of your legal writing with "WITNESSETH." Avoid using the word "said," as in "said agreement," "said injury," or "said accident." Avoid referring to the "underlying action." It is never clear to me when I see those words what the action is lying under. Avoid phrases such as "incumbent on me" or "I would be remiss." They make you sound pompous.

Also, avoid doubling or tripling up with words that are synonyms, such as "cease and desist," "each and every," "part and parcel," "terms and conditions," "null and void," "undertake and agree," "all and sundry," "due and payable," "goods and chattels," "possession, custody, or control," and "right, title, and interest." "Any and all" are not synonyms, but they regularly appear together as well. Why would you settle for just "any" when you can have "all," though? So just ask for "all." Use of these words was common in legal writing generations ago, and it still sneaks into our legal writing today. Their redundancy is unnecessary, however. If you reduce the number of words you use to describe the same thing, you'll have an easier time meeting the page limit for your brief.

Similarly, avoid the unnecessary use of Latin terms. No one outside of the Vatican speaks Latin, so unless you are writing to the College of Cardinals, use Latin terms sparingly. "Ad hoc," "alter ego," "de novo," "ex parte," "in pro per," and "pro se" are probably unavoidable. "A fortiori," "ab initio," "ad infinitum," "arguendo," "de facto," "in absentia," "ipse dixit," "ipso facto," "modus operandi," "nunc pro tunc," "persona non grata," "post hoc, ergo propter hoc," "sui generis," and "vel non" will only make you sound pretentious, if not overly proud that you took Latin in high school and aced it.

Finally, write in the active voice, as opposed to the passive, wherever possible. You would not say in real life, "A cheeseburger is wanted by me." You would say, "I want a cheeseburger." You would not say, "A trip to New York will be taken by me." Instead, you would say, "I will take a trip to New York." As ridiculous as the passive voice sounds when it is spoken, it is still used way too much in legal writing. "The statute was violated by the defendant." "A serious injury was suffered by the plaintiff." "Polluted water was leaked by the factory into the river."

On rare occasions, you will want to use the passive voice for emphasis. For example, "The plaintiff was fired for stealing" is more emphatic about the reason for the plaintiff's termination than "The employer fired the plaintiff for stealing." "The truck axle was removed for examination after the accident" is more emphatic regarding the suspected cause of the accident than "The company removed the truck axle for examination after the accident." If you have a good reason to use the passive voice in a particular sentence, use it. If you do not, try rewriting the sentence in the active voice. Your writing will be stronger. For example:

> "The company lost more than $100 million on the failed venture." versus
>
> "More than $100 million was lost by the company on the failed venture."

> "The company chose to file bankruptcy as a means to reorganize its finances." versus
>
> "Bankruptcy was chosen by the company as a means to reorganize its finances."

When you have finished your first draft of a legal document, go back over it and look for examples of archaic language, passive voice, pointless repetition, and useless legalese. Ask yourself, "Do people talk like this today?" If the answer is no, go back and update your language for the 21st century.

Write Economically

Always look for ways to express yourself using fewer words. You might have a 15-page limit for a brief, but if you can say it in 10 or 12 pages, your reader won't complain. How do you accomplish this?

First, eliminate unnecessary repetition. Too often I receive drafts of briefs that spend three paragraphs of the introduction telling me what happened in the case and then spend two more pages in the statement of facts telling me the same thing. You really only need to say it once.

Second, look for run-on sentences and break them up. If a sentence runs for more than three or four lines, it's probably too long. Sentences that go on and on are difficult to follow. When they are broken into smaller pieces, their meaning is much clearer, and you can usually eliminate a few words.

Third, focus only on the facts and law that are germane to your memo or brief. Unless you are writing or responding to a motion for summary judgment, not all of the facts of a case are relevant or need to be addressed. Limit your facts to those that bear on the issue at hand. Likewise, limit your discussion of the law to that which is most relevant to resolving the legal question or questions presented. Once you have answered the question, stop. Unless your assignment is specifically to leave no stone unturned, avoid spending time on throwaway arguments or issues. If the issue is whether an executive breached his employment agreement by working on a competing startup in his spare time, answer that question. Don't go off on a tangent speculating that the executive also might not have properly accounted for some sick days he took.

Fourth, tighten up your presentation by eliminating unnecessary words. Instead of saying "the instant case," simply say "this case." Say "after," not "subsequent to." Instead of saying "the defendant proceeded to download the documents," say "the defendant downloaded the documents." Instead of "the agency made the determination," say "the agency determined" or, better yet, "the agency decided." Instead of "the argument made by opposing counsel," say "opposing counsel's argument." Instead of "the Company was supportive of," say "the Company supported." You get the picture. By eliminating excess words, you will make your writing cleaner and easier for your reader to absorb. Your reader will be grateful, and you will start to build a reputation in your firm as an excellent writer.

Fifth, eliminate words such as "clearly," "obviously," and "undoubtedly." You don't add anything by saying "clearly, the plaintiff is wrong" instead of simply "the plaintiff is wrong." If in fact it's clear that the plaintiff is wrong, you weaken your argument by adding the extra word just to remind the reader. If it's not really clear, you damage your credibility with the reader by using the word to suggest that it is.

Mind Your Grammar and Usage

A review of applicable grammar and usage rules is beyond the scope of this book, but two good references are the classic Strunk & White, *The Elements of Style* (4th ed. 2003), and the more contemporary *Woe Is I* (3d ed. 2010) by Patricia T. O'Conner. Between the two books, they should be able to provide the answer to every grammar and usage question you might have (although they might not agree).

Your grammar likely will not be pristine. You might split an occasional infinitive or not always use the "Oxford comma." That's OK in most circumstances, so long as you do not make statements that are untrue or misleading due to grammatical errors or ambiguities, and so long as your variances from proper grammar and usage do not create distractions for your reader. Here are some grammar and usage errors that I often see that are both distracting and easily avoidable:

1. **Mixing present and past tense.** This often happens where the point headings (present tense) do not agree with the text that follows (past tense):

> **C. Plaintiff Resigns from Her Employment on Account of Harassment**
>
> On August 18, 2023, Plaintiff resigned. In her resignation letter, she said continued harassment by her manager was the reason for her quitting.

Sometimes there is tense disagreement within the paragraph itself as well:

C. Plaintiff Resigns from Her Employment on Account of Harassment

On August 18, 2023, Plaintiff resigned. In her resignation letter, she claims continued harassment by her manager was the reason for her quitting.

You must be consistent in your use of past or present tense. When you are telling a story, use of past tense is generally the better option.

2. Mixing singular and plural possessives. Where there is more than one defendant, you must refer to "Defendants' argument" consistently. You must not mix "Defendant's argument" and "Defendants' argument" in the same document. If you want to focus on one defendant's argument, you will need to be specific: "Defendant Brown's argument."

3. Use of ambiguous pronouns. If you say, "After Plaintiff reported Martin's harassment to David, he apologized and said it was just a misunderstanding," it is unclear whether it was Martin or David who apologized. Granted, you will want to use pronouns whenever you can to avoid repeating proper names excessively, but where an ambiguity exists, you must be more specific: "After Plaintiff reported Martin's harassment to David, Martin apologized and said it was just a misunderstanding."

4. Mixing up homophones. Homophones are words that are pronounced the same or similarly but are spelled differently and have different meanings. For example:

Advice vs. advise

Affect vs. effect

Allusion vs. illusion

Cite vs. site

Complement vs. compliment

Counsel vs. council

Discreet vs. discrete

Elicit vs. illicit

Ensure vs. insure

Immanent vs. imminent

Its vs. it's

Passed vs. past

Persecute vs. prosecute

Principal vs. principle

Respectively vs. respectfully

There vs. their vs. they're

To vs. too vs. two

Who's vs. whose

Your vs. you're

Be sure when you use one of these words that you are using the correct word. When in doubt, look it up!

5. Mixing up "e.g." and "i.e." E.g. stands for "exempli gratia" or "for example." Conversely, i.e. stands for "id est," which is Latin for "that is." They are not interchangeable.

6. Double negatives. Legal writing is hard enough to comprehend. The use of double negatives makes it that much more difficult. For example, "It's not untrue that the defendant agreed to forego further supporting the demonstrators." What does that sentence mean exactly? Double negatives are also weaker than their alternative: "I am not unmindful that my client testified" versus "I am aware that my client testified." "Meritless complaints of safety violations during a union organizing campaign are not uncommon" versus "Meritless complaints of safety violations during a union organizing campaign are common." You want to write from a position of strength, so avoid using double negatives in most instances. There might be times when a double negative is the best alternative, however. Your saying "We are not opposed to plaintiff's motion to continue the trial date" is not the same as saying "We are in favor of plaintiff's motion to continue the trial date." The former statement gives you room to maneuver should the plaintiff's requests for trial continuances become excessive. It's better to avoid a double negative, however, unless you have a specific reason to use it.

Use Consistent Citation Style

In most courts, use of the current edition of *The Bluebook: A Uniform System of Citation* is preferred, and in the U.S. Supreme Court and U.S. circuit courts of appeals, it is required. For many years, California courts required use of the *California Style Manual*, which differs from the *Bluebook* in many respects. Today, use of the *Bluebook* in California courts is permitted, although many state court judges in California still prefer use of the current edition of the *California Style Manual*, so the continued use of that manual is commonplace.

If you are required to use the *Bluebook* for a particular court filing, follow it carefully. If you are not required to use it—in writing briefs for lower courts, government agencies, arbitrators, mediators, clients, or opposing counsel, for example—following the *Bluebook* (or, in California, the *California Style Manual*) to the letter is less important, unless the partner you are working for was a member of the *Harvard Law Review*. Then, strict adherence to *Bluebook* style might be required. Otherwise, you need not spend hours obsessing over citation style, but you should ensure that your citation style is consistent. The purpose of standardized citation to cases and authorities is to identify the location of various laws and case language upon which you rely, without becoming a distraction to the reader.

You should always provide the full case citation when you first mention a case, listing the case name and a citation to at least one case reporter, including volume number, reporter edition, first page number of the case, court, and year of publication. For example: *Sharp v. S&S Activewear, LLC*, 69 F.4th 974 (9th Cir. 2023). For subsequent citations, list the case name (or an abbreviation) and the pincite (the page number where the quoted or cited language is found). For example: *Sharp v. S&S Activewear, supra*, 69 F.4th at 980, or simply *Sharp, supra*, 69 F.4th at 980. Other variations are commonly used too. What matters is that you stick with the same method throughout the document. Federal statutes should be cited as follows: 29 U.S.C. § 207. Federal regulations should be cited: 29 C.F.R. § 541.100. For state statutes, is it Cal. Labor Code, Cal. Lab. Code, or California Labor Code? It really doesn't matter, so long as you are consistent.

Don't Let Record Citations Get in the Way of Your Narrative

When you cite to the record of the case, put your citations in parentheses. Also, unless you are following *Bluebook* citation style closely, simplify those citations as much as possible. Otherwise, you will both exhaust and confuse your reader:

> General Manager Thomas testified that Plaintiff's poor attendance made it difficult for the engineering department at the Resort to function. Transcript of Deposition of Gregory Thomas at page 45, lines 3–11, attached as Exhibit C to Declaration of Linda Lawyer, filed herewith. Chief Engineer Sanchez disagreed, however. He testified that the department was usually able to cover for Plaintiff's absences without much consequence, and he referred to two weekly schedules as examples. Transcript of Deposition of Roberto Sanchez at page 67, lines 3–22 and Exhibits 12 and 13, attached as Exhibit D to Declaration of Linda Lawyer, filed herewith.

This reads much better:

> General Manager Thomas testified that Plaintiff's poor attendance made it difficult for the engineering department at the Resort to function. (Thomas Depo. 45:3–11.) Chief Engineer Sanchez disagreed, however. He testified that the engineering department was usually able to cover for Plaintiff's absences without much consequence, and he referred to two weekly schedules as examples. (Sanchez Depo. 67:3–22 & Exhs. 12–13.)

If you feel you need to say that the transcripts of the Thomas and Sanchez depositions are attached to the declaration of Ms. Lawyer, you could say it this way:

> General Manager Thomas testified that Plaintiff's poor attendance made it difficult for the engineering department at the

> Resort to function. (Thomas Depo. 45:3–11, Exh. C to Decl. of Linda Lawyer.) Chief Engineer Sanchez disagreed, however. He testified that the engineering department was usually able to cover for Plaintiff's absences without much consequence, and he referred to two weekly schedules as examples. (Sanchez Depo. 67:3–22 & Exhs. 12–13, Exh. D to Decl. of Linda Lawyer.)

Instead of repeating "Decl. of Linda Lawyer" twice in the paragraph, though, you could eliminate it from the citations to the depositions and drop a footnote at the end of the paragraph stating: "Cited excerpts of the transcripts of the Thomas and Sanchez depositions are attached as Exhibits C and D, respectively, to the Declaration of Linda Lawyer." Unorthodox? A bit, but the more important priority is to make a convincing argument that your reader can follow, not to fuss with a distracting tangle of record citations. Record citations in abbreviated form will still allow the reader to find the cited material in your papers. As with statutory and case citations, whichever format you choose to use for record citations, use it consistently throughout the document.

Proofread!

As emphasized throughout this book, proofreading your documents is essential. Submitting sloppy written work will derail your career as a law firm associate. You can use various online tools and AI applications to check your spelling, grammar, and syntax, but do not rely on those tools exclusively. You must still read and reread your work carefully to catch errors missed by your technology or errors created by your spell-checking program. Also, use your proofreading to ensure that your document reads smoothly, that your points are presented coherently and in order, and that transitions between paragraphs and sections of your document flow. Finally, proofread for tone. Is your tone appropriate? Especially if you wrote a motion or memo immediately following a particularly exasperating exchange with opposing counsel, your writing might contain some sharp edges that would be better sanded down. Remember my earlier point about attacking your opposing counsel's position or arguments without attacking him or her personally.

Don't just proofread a document from the beginning. Start proofreading halfway or two-thirds of the way through the document, and then go back to the beginning. You are more likely to find errors using that method than if you always proofread from the beginning of a document.

You should let your finished work set overnight if possible, so you can review it one last time with a fresh eye the next day. Not until you are certain it is correct, coherent, and complete should you submit it.

5

Pacing Yourself

One aspect of law firm life that many junior associates find challenging is managing their workload. To be fair, most associates' workloads are dictated primarily by the volume of the firm's work. When the firm is busy, associates will be busy. Star associates tend to be busier than other associates, moreover. It comes with the territory. The most successful associates in a law firm must be especially careful not to overload themselves to the point that their work quality suffers, however. This chapter will help you find the right balance.

Know How Your Firm Defines "Busy"

Your firm defines "busy" initially in terms of its annual billable and nonbillable hours targets. In some firms these targets are called "requirements," but whatever your firm calls them, you should meet or exceed them. Most firms have a target for billable hours and another target for nonbillable but valuable time, such as training time, pro bono work, service on firm committees, and client development tasks such as writing articles, assisting with conference presentations, and so on. Some firms have a target for billable hours and for total hours, which include nonbillable time such that you can exceed the whole target with just billable hours if you have them.

Your firm also defines "busy" in terms of the level of your engagement in the firm's work. The volume of work in most law firms is somewhat variable, but when the firm is busy, it will expect you to pull your weight and more. Law practice is not a 40-hour-per-week profession. If the firm is very busy and you come in after 9 a.m. and leave at 5 p.m., it will be noticed. You must arrange your personal life such that when the firm needs you to be working, you can show up and focus. Late nights and/or weekends might be required for you to keep up with the pace. It's part of law firm life.

Your firm will probably have peaks and valleys in its workload, so there will be times when you will not need to work long hours. It is precisely because of these peaks and valleys, however, that you must take advantage of the busy times to advance you toward your firm's hours targets. If extra billable hours are available early in the year, be sure to work them. The volume of work might decline as you approach the finish line. Especially if your firm's measuring year ends on December 31, you cannot count on making up for lost time during the last two weeks of the year. Most lawyers, and most clients, will be off celebrating the holidays. If you are short on hours at the beginning of December, you will likely be shorter on hours at the end of December.

You must keep track of your progress toward your firm's hours targets throughout the year, therefore. Most firms make this information easily accessible, but if you are unclear about where to find it, ask. If you monitor your progress during the year and plan your work accordingly, you should be OK. If you find yourself falling short along the way, that's the time to fix it. Let partners with whom you have worked well know that you have availability. Also let your office managing partner know, as well as your team leader if you have one and your mentor(s). Don't be afraid to say that your workload is running low. A star associate with availability is music to the ears of every law firm partner. Speak up and you will soon have an abundance of work again.

Understanding Deadlines

A common mistake of new lawyers is misunderstanding deadlines. A brief or discovery responses might be due on Friday, but you cannot wait until Thursday night to produce a draft. This is because the partner must review the draft and then the client will likely need to review it as well before it is filed or served. All of this cannot occur in a couple of hours. You must know, therefore, how long the partner will need to review the document and how long the client representative will need as well. You should add an extra day for contingencies, then combine the client review time and the partner review time, plus the extra day, and that will be your deadline for producing a draft of the document (in Chapter 4 we covered the fact that a "draft" in legal parlance is not really a "draft" as you might have understood the word before you started your legal career). You must not think of the due date for a document as being the same thing as your deadline. Your deadline might be several days or a week in advance of the due date. Plan accordingly. If you are unclear on your deadline for any assignment, simply ask the partner, "When do you want this back from me?"

Keep Your Pipeline Full

Star associates remain busy despite the ebbs and flows of the firm's workload. They manage to do so by always keeping their pipeline full. Many times I have received an email from within the firm announcing that one associate or another has "settled all of her cases" and has time available. Those associates are rarely star associates because they do not know how to manage their workload. Many associates fall prey to thinking that because they are slammed this week, they are too busy to take on any more assignments. That is short-sighted and incorrect thinking. If I come to you to ask you to work on a new lawsuit with me, you might think you cannot possibly take on any more work at the moment, but that's not what I am asking. I am offering you a stream of work that will last six months to two years or more. Nothing has to be done today. Over the next week I would like for you to take time to read the complaint and have a discussion with me about what we will submit as our initial responsive pleading, but that's all of your time I will need this week.

You always must be looking at your pipeline beyond this week. What does it look like for the next month? The next three months? The next six months? You should keep track of your pipeline in writing so you can keep it full. If it's only in your head, it will always seem overwhelming. Some associates use a whiteboard in their office to keep track of their work assignments and deadlines; others keep track electronically. Do whatever works for you, but chart out your key deadlines so you can see them in front of you. Look for periods of time when you will not be so busy, and look for opportunities to fill that time. It will not work out perfectly. Many things in law practice happen quickly and without warning, so you may frequently have to juggle priorities. You will be looking ahead, however, not just at your current workload, and that should allow you to keep your pipeline full so you will remain consistently busy.

Don't Overcommit

When I was a young associate, the founder of my law firm called me in for a chat. That was hardly ever a good sign, so I was more than a little apprehensive. It went OK, though. We had a good talk about my experience as an associate so far, and he closed the discussion with this piece of advice: "Don't overcommit yourself. It's better to do an excellent job on a few assignments than really screw up a lot of assignments." It was good advice then, and it remains good advice now.

You might be thinking, "You were just telling me I need to stay busy all the time, but now you're telling me not to overcommit!" It's not inconsistent, though. There's a difference between staying busy and overcommitting. Overcommitting is taking on another motion for summary judgment that's due within a couple of days of the due date for a motion for summary judgment you already have, and that's due the day before the due date for an appellate brief you are working on. If you keep track in writing of your key deadlines, you can prevent this from happening. Moreover, if a partner seems irritated that you cannot take on his motion for summary judgment, explain to him the deadlines you are facing already in the same time frame. Most partners know that if they insist you take the assignment nonetheless, the work product they get will not be good, and they would rather find another associate who has the bandwidth to take on the project. They might not seem thrilled about your not being able to work with them, but they'll get over it, especially if you have a reputation as a hardworking associate and you are already well on pace to exceed your billable hours target for the year.

Some associates take this advice too far, though. Two motions for summary judgment and an appellate brief all due within a three-day period are too much. Interrogatories to be answered and two research projects to complete all in the same week present a different picture. You could probably stretch those three assignments to fill a week of billable hours, but you will not win the respect of a partner whose additional assignment you turn down. You must be open to taking on another assignment even if it requires you to push yourself a bit to get everything done. You will push yourself for your entire legal career. It's how you become more efficient and how you overcome smaller challenges that prepare you for larger ones.

Don't Panic If You're Not Always Busy

What if the opposite occurs? What if you have a week with no deadlines on your whiteboard and little or no work? You told your mentors and the partners you work with that you are light on work, yet still no new assignments. Some associates panic in such a scenario, but you should not. Celebrate it! Take a long weekend away with your significant other, visit your family, or visit an old friend to catch up. Take a trip on your own to a place you've been wanting to visit. Even if you don't leave town, take some time off to attend a play or concert, see a movie, go shopping, or have a spa day. Live like a normal person, however briefly. The work will pick back up eventually. It always does.

You must pace yourself in your legal career. Much of your work as an associate in a law firm will involve high stress. Great lawyers take the stress in stride, but they are able to do so because they take advantage of downtime to relax and refresh, to step off the treadmill for a few days to live life more slowly for a bit. This is another skill you will need to master along your own path toward becoming a great lawyer.

6

Take the Initiative

One of the most common complaints of partners about associates is that they only do what they are asked. It's certainly important to do what you are asked and to do a terrific job at that. That's only a part of what makes a star associate, though. What distinguishes the star associate from other associates is that the star associate does not merely perform assigned tasks but is always anticipating what he or she can do next to move the case further toward a resolution or the transaction toward closing, to advance the firm, or to further develop his or her career.

Offer, Don't Wait to Be Asked

Partners are usually very busy. They can be pulled in several different directions at once and find it hard to focus. Details can sometimes slip through the cracks. You are the associate working on the case. You probably know the case better than the partner knows it by now. You know what needs to be done next. Partners love it when you offer to do the next thing that must be done in the case, rather than waiting for the partner to ask you to do so. They *really* love it when you just go ahead and perform the next task without waiting to be asked. For example, after you have finished drafting the answer and affirmative defenses, if you know the partner will want to send out an initial round of written discovery, you draft it without waiting for the partner to ask. Or when the answers to that written discovery come in, if you know the partner will want to see the plaintiff's medical records, you issue a subpoena for them before the partner requests that you do so. When in doubt, ask the partner if you should perform a particular task, but if you are just taking the next step in what you know is the partner's preferred method for managing a case, you likely will be safe in taking the initiative.

There are many tasks you can perform without being asked for which the partner will be grateful. When you start working on a newly filed case, look on the court's website to see if the assigned judge has any special rules or procedures. Some judges, for example, want attorneys to appear only virtually for nonevidentiary hearings. Other judges insist on in-person appearances unless leave is granted to appear virtually. Some judges require that courtesy copies of pleadings and briefs filed electronically be delivered to their chambers. Most federal judges and some state court judges require that a specific procedure be followed for resolving discovery disputes. If the judge has special requirements or procedures, alert the partner so that you both can be prepared to comply. Many lawyers never bother to check to see if a judge has any additional requirements. If you check to find out, and if you and your firm comply with those requirements, the judge will know you are paying attention, and you are more likely to get what you need from the court. Also, conduct some basic research on the judge's background. If you find anything indicating possible bias or a conflict of interest, alert the partner right away.

If the new case is venued in an unfamiliar jurisdiction, review the court's local rules. Make note of any special requirements and if there are any, alert the partner and her assistant. Some courts, for example, require counsel to "meet and confer" prior to filing a motion to dismiss or strike a complaint as your initial responsive pleading. If you fail to complete this step, your motion could be denied. Some courts impose limits on how long parties may stipulate to extend a defendant's deadline to respond to a complaint.

Some state courts impose lengthy requirements on counsel, similar to those under Federal Rule 26, to meet and coordinate to file a joint initial case management report. If the jurisdiction has any of these requirements, your learning about them at the outset and alerting others working on the case with you will avert embarrassment, an unsuccessful motion, or sanctions later.

When opposing counsel's responses to the written discovery you prepared come in, review them and make a list of any deficiencies. Share the list with the partner and obtain the partner's guidance on how to address the deficiencies. In most jurisdictions there is a time limit for you to file a motion to compel further discovery and a "meet and confer" process that must precede any such motion. Don't be like most lawyers and wait until the deadline for a motion is only a few days away to review your opponent's responses and begin the "meet and confer" process. An early review will give the partner enough time to consider the responses and consult with the client to determine their preference on how to proceed, and it will give you enough time to write a first-rate motion to compel further responses if that's the client's chosen path.

If a deposition is approaching, unless you are sure that the partner has done so, remind the client representative that the deposition is approaching and that he or she is welcome to attend. A good way to really irritate a client is to take a key deposition in a case and forget to invite the client. The same goes for individually named defendants in a case. They have the right to be present at depositions, and if your firm is jointly representing them with the corporate client, your firm has an obligation to keep them apprised of key events in the case. Invite the individual defendants to the deposition. While you're at it, confirm that a court reporter has been arranged for the deposition, as well as a videographer and an interpreter if needed.

Similarly, if a case is going to mediation, offer to prepare a draft case analysis (aka liability analysis or exposure analysis) for the client and the insurance carrier if one is involved. This case analysis is essential for the client representative and/or claims manager to assess potential exposure in the case and obtain sufficient settlement authority for the mediation. That process takes time. Clients and insurers hate it when they are reminded at the last minute about a mediation of which they have only a vague recollection of approving months ago but have not thought about since. You can prevent such a debacle by preparing a draft case analysis[8] well in advance of the mediation date and by providing a reminder about the mediation date as the date draws nearer.

When a case settles, take responsibility for ensuring that the settlement is completed. A settlement agreement must be prepared and signed by the parties. See to it that all parties who need to sign the settlement agreement actually do so. Determine which entity will be responsible for the settlement payment, obtain W-9 forms from the payees, and forward the forms to the payor of the settlement payment. Follow up to ensure that the settlement payment is made on or before the deadline. Once the settlement payment has been made, ensure that the required documentation is filed to effect a dismissal of the case with prejudice.

Outside of the litigation context, too, you can offer to assist in ways for which the partner will be grateful. Say you are on a call with the partner and a client about a complicated issue and it becomes apparent that more legal analysis must be done before the client will be comfortable making a decision. After the call concludes, offer to do the research and produce a memo on what you find before the partner has an opportunity to ask you. Likewise, perhaps a partner is committed to making a presentation to an important client, to an industry association, or at an ABA meeting. Offer to conduct some background research on the topic of the presentation and to assist in creating the PowerPoint slides for the presentation.

8. The partner will need to see and approve this analysis before you send it to the client and/or insurer.

The more you offer to perform tasks that you know must be done before you are asked to perform them, the more valuable partners in your firm will find you. Anticipating what needs to be done and just doing it is not difficult, but in an environment in which everyone else is waiting to be told what to do next, you will really stand out. You will be known as the associate who has the partners' backs, and that's a great attribute!

Ask for Opportunities

Many associates simply do their work and wait until they are asked to take the next step up in their career. But why wait to be asked? Why not ask instead? Ask to work on the interesting new case that just came in. Ask to take some depositions, to handle a hearing, or to second-chair a trial. Ask to handle a government investigation or the negotiation of a simple transaction. By simply asking for the opportunity, you might get it. If you do not, don't be discouraged. Maybe the client expects that only the partner will take depositions, handle hearings, or negotiate transactions. Maybe the partner thinks you are just not yet ready. Stay on your path of superior performance, and the partner will think you are ready before much longer.

Always be on the lookout for opportunities to grow, to challenge yourself. Sometimes they will appear when you least expect them. As an associate I second-chaired a weeklong bench trial in federal court in Miami. I examined a minor witness or two, but the partner handled most of the trial. The judge ordered us to come back and finish up our last witness on Saturday morning. We finished the witness, and then the partner asked the judge's clerk about what briefing schedule the judge might prefer. The clerk responded, "Briefing schedule? The court will hear closing arguments this morning." The partner had not planned to present a closing argument and began to panic. I offered to do the closing, and she gratefully agreed. I quickly scribbled an outline for the closing, stood up and argued our case, and the court ruled from the bench in our favor. Some lawyers have to wait years for such an opportunity. Others step up to the challenge when it appears. Litigation always throws you curveballs. Don't be afraid to offer to take a swing if you are reasonably confident that you can hit the ball.

Volunteer

Another way to be proactive is to offer to write or coauthor articles for the firm's website or client newsletters. Such articles will highlight your expertise to audiences within and outside of the firm. If your firm presents seminars or presentations for clients and prospects, look for opportunities to volunteer to participate. Even if you do not get a speaking role in the presentation, you might meet lawyers from other offices, and your interest and hard work will put you at the head of the line for a more visible role in future presentations.

Look for opportunities to volunteer in your own office as well. Many firms have associates assist with recruiting of other associates for an office. Volunteering for such an activity will expose you to partners and associates in your office you might not know well and give you a head start toward becoming familiar with the firm's new hires in your office. Firms might offer opportunities as well to serve on office committees focused on social events, space planning, or marketing and business development. Those opportunities can help you develop leadership skills, and star associates are almost always leaders in their firms.

Become an Expert

Law firms need experts in practice areas who are knowledgeable enough that they can serve as a resource to other lawyers in the firm. Becoming a subject-matter expert takes work. You must really master the area of law. Emerging areas of law or new regulations will be your best bets because they are brand new. You will not need to absorb decades of prior analysis of an older law. A new law might not be game changing, but if it affects your firm's clients, it will be worth your effort in mastering it.

When I was an associate, Congress enacted the Worker Adjustment and Retraining Notification Act (WARN Act). It required that companies closing plants or laying off a substantial number of employees provide at least 60 days advance notice to affected employees. Like most legislation, it included some complicated definitions and exceptions. I do not now recall whether I volunteered or *was* volunteered, but I became my firm's first expert on the WARN Act while still an associate. I received inquiries from all over the firm about the new law, and I continued to receive those inquiries for years, long after becoming a partner even. Not only did it result in billable work, but it also helped me to establish a positive reputation in the eyes of partners and other colleagues who did not otherwise know me.

Find your WARN Act. Study it thoroughly and understand its practical implications for your firm's clients. Once you feel confident in your knowledge of the new law, let it be known around the firm that you are interested in it and have mastered it. Perhaps write an article for a firm publication or the firm's website. Offer to present a webinar or an internal seminar. As it becomes known that you can serve as a resource for others in your firm, be responsive when they reach out to you to ask you for assistance or for more details. It will be just one more reason that others in the firm will come to regard you as a star associate.

7

Remember, You Are Working for a Client

The word "client" does not come up very often in most law schools. It's almost as if the whole world of law exists without those pesky people who pay the bills. The only exception is in the professional responsibility course where the word "client" is mentioned occasionally, but only in terms of the minimal ethical duties owed to the client—don't steal from your client, don't represent clients with competing interests, don't forget to tell your client about that settlement offer. No part of the course is spent on how to provide excellent client service. Some law schools offer clinical experiences where you might have a real client who is seeking immigration asylum or attempting to overturn a criminal conviction, but those clients are very different from the clients you will serve as a lawyer in a business law firm.

The clients you will represent hire law firms to solve business problems for them. Since you are a lawyer, you might think it's a legal problem, but to the client it's a business problem. The problem might involve the defense of a lawsuit or government investigation. It might involve the prosecution of a lawsuit against a competitor, a vendor, a customer, another business, or a former employee acting unlawfully or in breach of contract. It might involve assisting the client to comply with a particular law or regulation. It might involve guiding the client toward the closing of a complicated financial transaction. Whatever the problem, you must understand that the client sees it through a business lens. With rare exceptions, the client is not interested in making new law. The client wants to solve a problem. It will be up to your law firm to ensure that the client's business goals are met as you solve the problem. Even as a junior associate you will play a role in helping the client achieve its business goals, but first you must understand the client's goals.

Know Your Client

Before you can fully understand your client's business goals, you have to understand your client. Essentially, you have two clients: the client organization that your firm represents and to which it owes various ethical duties, and the client representative who oversees the relationship between the client organization and your firm. There might be more than one client representative for a particular client organization, but one of them is likely to have the final say. In a larger corporation, this person is likely to be the general counsel or an associate or assistant general counsel in charge of the area of the law in which you practice, such as litigation, securities law, environmental law, or employment law. Where the client does not have an internal general counsel, its client representative might be the chief executive officer, the chief financial officer, or another executive officer. To understand your client, you must become familiar with both the client organization and the client representative.

The Client Organization

The more you know about the client organization, the better positioned you will be to understand its business goals. You can obtain an introduction initially by viewing the client's website to give you an idea of the products or services it provides, the markets it serves, and the locations of its operations. While the website is a good start, the knowledge of the client that will be more important to you will be the knowledge you absorb as you perform work for the client. You will absorb this knowledge only if you pay attention, though. Many associates simply move from one assignment to the next without knowing much about the client or its objectives. This might be unavoidable if you are only asked to perform a discrete research assignment for a client, but if you find yourself performing work for a client on a more regular basis, you should attempt to learn as much about the client as you can.

The first thing you should try to learn about a client organization is what unique challenges it faces. Is it experiencing financial headwinds? Is it growing faster than its existing infrastructure can support? Is it facing labor relations conflicts? Is it a party to a substantial amount of litigation? Is it trying to capture market share in a ruthlessly competitive industry? Is it the focus of government regulators? Is it an acquisition target or is it seeking to grow by acquisitions? These and other challenges will help to define the type of work your firm will perform for the client and how the client will expect that work to be carried out. For example, will the client be budget conscious or want to win at any cost? The more you understand about the client's current challenges, the better you will perform if you become part of that client's team at your firm.

Second, what does the client look to your firm to do for it? Does it rely on your firm for legal services in a variety of areas, or does it assign your firm only matters in a specific area or areas? Many corporate general counsel will say they hire lawyers, not law firms, meaning they seek to retain the top legal talent regardless of the law firm where that talent may be located. Other client organizations rely on one firm or a small number of firms for most of their legal services, preferring the familiarity of a trusted advisor. As a member of a client team in your firm, you should understand your firm's mission with respect to that client. Was your firm hired to take a specific case to trial and win it, or does the client look to your firm for broader advice about the matters assigned, such as whether an early resolution would be beneficial, how a public lawsuit might affect the organization's brand, and what steps might be taken to avoid similar exposure in the future?

Third, you should learn the structure of your firm's relationship with the client. Is the partner in charge of the client relationship the only lawyer in your firm who communicates directly with the client, or do communications flow from multiple representatives of the client to various lawyers in your firm? Is the client OK with your contacting its executives and managers directly to obtain information or documents you need, or does the client want you to go through a gatekeeper? If you are permitted to contact client executives and managers directly, are you expected to copy an associate general counsel? Most large organizations have protocols they will want you to follow so they can manage communications into and out of the organization. Learn the client's protocol and follow it.

Fourth, you should know how the client evaluates your firm's work. If your firm handles a volume of cases for the client, does the client measure your firm's per-claim expense data or time toward resolution for each claim? Or does the client take a more holistic approach where it is generally satisfied if legal matters are being handled well and costs are not excessive? If the client is using metrics to evaluate your firm's performance, know the metrics and always be thinking about how your handling of a case will affect your firm's metrics. If the metrics favor cost control, you should always be looking for the most economical resolution of a case. If the metrics favor prompt resolution of claims, try not to let your case drag on.

Finally, you should learn about the client's culture. Is it buttoned-up and conservative or entrepreneurial and freewheeling? Is the management structure hierarchical or flat? If you visit the client's site for meetings, get a feel for the working atmosphere. Do the client's employees have fun while they are working, or are they all business? Do they enjoy the company of their lawyers, or do they consider you a distraction? In a privately held company, is the founder still active in the business? Many such companies reflect the values of the founder. Such values might emphasize frugality, treating employees well, or community involvement. If you can identify the values that guide the organization, you will be better able to serve it.

Don't make assumptions about what a client's culture might be like, however. As a young lawyer I was privileged to be on a team serving a client that was remaking an entire industry. Working on that team was a 24/7 commitment. I was taken off the team, though, because the client perceived that I was too intense and did not have a sense of humor. (That was a long time ago.) I learned a lot from that experience. Not all clients are a good fit for every lawyer, and you won't know about a client's culture until you experience it. Once you understand the client's culture, you will want to do your best to fit in, but if you are not a good fit, don't sweat it. Simply learn from the experience and move on.

The Client Representative

If you have direct access to the client, it likely will be through a particular client representative. You should learn as much as you can about that person and his or her preferences for working with outside counsel. Does the client representative primarily supervise outside counsel, or does she have a full portfolio of other executive responsibilities in addition to working with counsel? Does he want to review every brief or significant correspondence before it goes out, or is he happy with your simply keeping him in the loop? Does she have authority to settle cases, or does she need to obtain that authority from her superiors or from the leader of the business unit involved? Does he travel frequently, such that he might be difficult to reach when you need him to review a document?

Also learn as much as you can about your client representative's work style. Avoid asking personal questions about family commitments and the like, especially early in the relationship, but observe what you can. Does she leave the office promptly at a particular time every day? Does she email you on Saturday mornings or Sunday afternoons? Does he offer you his personal cell number and tell you it's OK to call after hours if necessary? Is he OK with text messaging? Some client representatives work virtually all the time. Others have more balanced lives. Whatever their work style, you will want to interact with them consistent with that style and not disrupt their lives with emails at odd hours or late submission of documents for their review.

Finally, try to learn what is expected of your client representative by his or her boss. If the client organization works hard to control legal costs, your client representative will probably be evaluated at least in part on how well he manages costs in the matters he supervises. If that's the case, you will want to keep the costs in your matter under control and let him know you are thinking about it. Ask him, for example, if he thinks it's really necessary to take nonparty witness depositions before mediation or whether it might make sense to postpone them and save some money. Other client organizations might not be so focused on costs, but the general counsel might make it clear she does not like surprises. You would want to correspond in more detail with such a client about every step in the case than you might with a client who is not so detail oriented. One of your firm's objectives is to make your client representative look good to his or her boss, and you have an important role in making that happen.

Know How Your Client Defines a "Win"

Lawyers like to win. Less competitive people tend to choose other professions. Lawyers love to win the cases they litigate. Sometimes we are fortunate enough to get a case dismissed on a Rule 12(b)(6) motion or win a motion for summary judgment. Even so, the other side might appeal. If an early disposition of the case is not in the cards, a trial on the merits, usually before a jury, will be necessary in order to put a win on the board, and again the losing party might well appeal. In some cases, the opponent does not give up until the U.S. Supreme Court hears the case or denies certiorari. In most cases, however, your client will have no interest in going to the Supreme Court. In fact, most corporate clients will not want to take a case through a jury trial unless all reasonable efforts to settle the case have been exhausted. Most clients will not want to incur the expense of a trial and will not want to take the risk that a runaway jury will take the opportunity to hit a "big corporation" with a large verdict. The negative publicity that comes from an adverse jury verdict is not helpful toward promoting the client's brand, either.

When a client assigns your firm a new case, therefore, they will likely define a "win" as something different than a Supreme Court ruling in their favor five or more years down the road. You must understand how the client defines the win in each case you work on, as a frequent client complaint is that their lawyers are not aligned with their goals in a particular matter. If you are unclear, ask the partner on the case. Often when you are defending a lawsuit, the client will define a win as the most economical resolution possible of the case, taking into account the settlement amount and legal fees and costs. This requires judgment on the part of the defense lawyer regarding the optimal time to seek a resolution. If you wait too long, defense costs will be high, and opposing counsel's investment in the case will be substantial as well, driving up settlement expectations. If you settle too early before the plaintiff's deposition is taken and the facts are clear, on the other hand, you might overpay. With experience you will be able to find the optimal point for resolution of most cases, but when you are still learning, this is a topic you will want to discuss with the lead partner.

Sometimes a client's definition of a win changes over the course of a case. The goal starting out might be to teach a competitor a lesson about stealing trade secrets, but as costs mount and the evidence turns out not to be what it had seemed initially, the goal might shift toward finding a resolution that will end the litigation while still making a point. In another case, the initial goal might be to defend a case aggressively to take a stand against frivolous lawsuits, but should a key witness disappear or change her testimony, the client's goal might change to cutting its losses. Similarly, in a nonlitigation setting, a client might hire your firm to handle the acquisition of a smaller company, but due diligence might reveal good reasons not to complete the transaction, and the client's goal might shift to exiting the transaction with minimal exposure. As an associate, you might not be a part of the conversation between the client and the partner in charge of the matter regarding the initial definition of the "win" and changes in that definition as the case or transaction progresses, but it's important that you communicate with the partner about this subject so that your work remains aligned with the client's goals. Moreover, should you discover a problem in a case or transaction that might cause the client to want to change its initial goal, bring it to the partner's attention right away. The client might not be happy to hear the bad news, but they will not blame you or your law firm unless you fail to raise it in a timely fashion.

Provide Five-Star Client Service in a 2½-Star World

In recent years, we have experienced a reduced level of customer service from many industries. "Yes, sir, we have a hotel room for you, but we no longer offer in-room dining, and housekeeping will cost extra." We must tag and check our own bags at the airport, and the only difference if you fly first or business class is that there is a special line for you. In an increasing number of restaurants (not just fast food), we must order our food at the counter and sometimes pick it up there too. We often must check out our own groceries. We get used to it. What are you going to do? But then we have an outstanding customer service experience in a hotel, restaurant, airport, or store. We are wowed, and we ask, "Why can't every hotel/restaurant/airline/store be like this?" The answer is that, while many of them would like to be, they cannot find enough employees who are willing and able to deliver such a high level of customer service on a consistent basis.

The same goes for law firms. Not every lawyer or law firm has a customer service mentality, and only a small handful of them seem to understand its importance. Lawyers will usually try to meet clients' stated expectations, but even that can be spotty. *Exceeding* a client's expectations is rarely part of the conversation in a law firm.

There is an opportunity in this for you. As you begin your career in law, recognize that you are in the customer service business and that you just happen to be a lawyer, too. This is the mindset of the profession's most successful business developers. If you orient yourself in this way from the beginning, you won't have to retrain yourself later.

Let's start with what *not* to do. Don't be fake. I cringe every time I read an associate's email to a client they do not know that starts with "I hope you had a nice weekend." Even worse, "I hope you have a nice weekend," and it's only *Wednesday*! And it's not Thanksgiving! The client knows you don't really care about their weekend. You are just wasting time and space. It's different if you have established a relationship with a client and you actually know something about what they did over the weekend. If you know they went skiing, by all means ask them on Monday or Tuesday about their ski trip. That's the kind of question that will strengthen your connection with a client representative. Unless you can make an authentic personal inquiry of the client, however, it's best to skip the weekend words and just get to the point.

So what *should* you do to provide five-star client service?

First, be super-responsive. Many clients have become accustomed to attorneys taking a long time to return calls and respond to emails. I am amazed at how many of my clients say, "Thank you for returning my call so quickly" or "Thanks for your prompt response" to their email. I actually thought that was my job. Apparently, their other lawyers are not as fast to respond. When you receive a call or email from a client, make it a priority to respond as soon as you can. The client reached out to you because they need something. They didn't just call to say hello. The sooner you give them what they need, the sooner they can solve their problem and move on to the next one. If you absolutely cannot provide an answer to the client's question right away, at least contact the client to acknowledge that you have their message and will respond as soon as you finish a meeting or deposition. Then, get back to the client as soon as you are free. Your prompt response will distinguish you from all of the other lawyers from whom your client is still waiting for return calls or emails, and that is a big win for you.

You'll get even more points from your client if you respond promptly to their emails received after hours or on a weekend or if you indicate your availability for a telephone conference about an urgent issue on a weekend. I once cemented a relationship with an important client by being available for her on Saturday afternoons. That's when she caught up on emails and phone calls left over from a busy week. I made sure to respond promptly to her emails as I received them on Saturdays, and she knew she could call me if it was easier than emailing about a particular issue. If I happened to miss a Saturday because of another commitment, it was OK, but she really appreciated that I was available to work with her most Saturdays to resolve outstanding issues when she had the time to do so. You might be thinking, "But my Saturdays are my time." They are, and there are law jobs that provide predictable hours and weekends off. Those jobs do not typically include working in a large law firm, however. Serving busy client executives is not a 9 to 5, Monday through Friday endeavor. Star associates recognize this and make themselves available when their clients need them.

Second, give the client your cell phone number. If it's possible to include your cell phone number on your email signature, do so, and let the client know they are free to call you on your cell if necessary. If it's not on your email signature, give it to the client at an appropriate time. Not right away, but after you have communicated with them a bit. A good time is when you send them a document to review, especially if a weekend is approaching. Tell them, "Call me on my cell if that's more convenient." Don't be surprised if the client calls you. Consider it not an interruption of your personal time but rather an opportunity to connect with the client at a time convenient for them. The client will appreciate your flexibility and remember your client service orientation.

By the way, if you are going to make your cell phone number available to clients, consider getting a number that is local to your office. Switching cell phone numbers is usually fairly easy. Even if there is a cost involved, it's a worthwhile investment. If you are based in your firm's Los Angeles office but you still have the suburban Atlanta cell phone number you had in high school, it can be confusing to a client. You want the client to think of you potentially for future assignments in California, not be wondering if you might actually be located in Atlanta, so get a number with a Los Angeles area code. An out-of-state area code can also be confusing to prospective clients you might meet locally. You will want to give the impression that you are committed to remaining in the area, not that you might just be there temporarily.

Third, don't just meet client deadlines, beat them. If a client tells you she needs to have a brief or other document for review at least 24 hours before it's due, give it to her at least 48 hours in advance. Your client representative is likely very busy, and things come up unexpectedly. At those times she will appreciate your giving her more time than she requested to review a document, and you will again be distinguished from the other lawyers with whom she works. To beat a client's deadline, you simply need to schedule your work on the project to conclude a day earlier. This will not be a hardship for you if you plan accordingly (we covered this in Chapter 5).

Fourth, get to know the client's business. Do as much as you can to improve your familiarity with the client's business. You don't want to waste your client representative's time asking questions about the organization that can be answered easily from a review of its website or other accessible public sources, but asking a question or two for more factual background on an issue you are currently working on will show the client that you are interested in learning more about its business. The problems you will work on likely will be the result of factors not apparent on the client's website, such as integration difficulties following a merger, a government investigation triggered by political pressure from a competitor, or disruptions in production caused by supply chain breakdowns. The client will not consider your desire to learn more about these challenges to be a waste of time.

Also, get to know the language of your client's industry. An organization of doctors is called a "practice" or perhaps a "clinic" but not a "partnership," even though the doctors are likely partners. If it's a large organization that provides anesthesiology, radiology, or pathology services to hospitals, it's probably called a "group." An organization of attorneys, accountants, architects, or engineers is typically called a "firm," not a "company," even though it might be incorporated. In the hospitality business, a hotel is often called a "property," not a "hotel," unless it's a "resort." Resorts are hotels plus golf, tennis, spas, restaurants, and the like. Restaurants and bars in hotels often are called "outlets." A retail seller of automobiles and trucks is called a "dealership." What used to be called a "warehouse" is now a "distribution center." What used to be called a "trucking company" is now often called a "logistics company," although in the transportation industry, trucking companies, airlines, and railroads are also called "carriers." In the insurance industry, insurance companies are called "carriers," too.[9] Learn the lingo for your client's industry. It will signal to your client that you "get it."

In addition, if you are representing businesses, consider regularly reading business publications such as *The Wall Street Journal*. They are excellent sources of business news, and invariably your clients or their industries are likely to be mentioned in their articles, which can be good conversation starters. It will not hurt you to say to a client, "I read in this morning's *Wall Street Journal* . . . ." It will confirm for your client that you are interested in their business and industry, not just in billing hours.

9. Because they "carry" the risk of their insureds.

Client site visits are less common now in the age of Zoom and Teams, but if you get an opportunity to visit a client site, seize it. Demonstrate in person your interest in learning more about the client's operations and culture. Especially if the client is in manufacturing, logistics, or research and development, ask for a tour of their facility. I have made such requests throughout my career, and no client has ever refused. They will bring out the special visitor's safety vest and hard hat for you, and they will proudly show off their operation. You can learn a lot on these tours. Not just about how the client designs, makes, or moves product, but about the employee culture at the company. Are the employees smiling and friendly? Do they greet the manager who is escorting you around, or do they tend to avoid him or her? Make mental notes about all you observe. *Never bill the client for the plant tour, however.* Whatever goodwill you generated by taking the plant tour will be lost when the client receives the invoice.

Fifth, give the client exactly what it needs. Because you have taken the time to get to know the client's business, and the preferences of the client representative for working with outside counsel, you are equipped to provide the service that is focused on what the client needs. If the client is under pressure to save money on legal spend and expects your law firm to partner with it to keep costs down, write a brief email rather than a formal memorandum to answer the questions posed to you. If the client is struggling to hire and retain enough employees to staff its growing operations, keep this consideration in mind as you answer questions the client poses to you. Sometimes the strictly legal answer is not the best answer when placed in the context of the client's current business challenges.[10] In any event, provide a clear answer when the client asks you a question. If the answer depends on which facts are

10. For example, suppose a client asks you whether state law requires that employees' unused sick days be paid out at the end of the year. You do your research and find that the answer is no. You can simply tell the client the answer is no. Better yet, you could tell the client that while the answer is no, they might want to consider paying for the unused sick days to prevent numerous employees from calling out sick in the last few weeks of the year.

presented or on the outcome of a pending appellate court case, say so and present the likely alternatives. Don't be evasive or just conclude that the answer is "not clear." If that's the best you can do, the client is likely to ask the same question of another law firm to see if it can find more clarity.

Sixth, keep the client informed about important developments in the law affecting it. Clients appreciate your informing them of new legal developments affecting their business. The client will probably know about major legislation or court decisions directly affecting its industry, so your joining the other two dozen or so law firms highlighting those same obvious items for the client will produce negligible benefit. Look instead for new cases or regulations that might affect the client in a way they might not have anticipated. An example might be a regulation or court ruling requiring accommodation of neurodivergent persons in the health care setting. If your client operates retail stores, you might bring the new regulation to their attention, pointing out that although now the focus of the regulation or court ruling is on health care, it might easily extend later to other forms of public accommodation. Your client will appreciate your looking out for them. As with the plant tour, moreover, don't bill the client for notifying them about a new development in the law unless it directly impacts a case or matter you are actively handling for the client. Consider it a *lagniappe*, as they say in New Orleans. A little something extra.

8

Going to Court

You've probably been to court a few times with a partner or senior associate. Now you are about to make your first court appearance on your own. This is what you always wanted when you decided to become a lawyer. You might be a bit anxious about it, but it will go fine if you follow a few basic rules.

Dress for Success

Wear a business suit, no exceptions. Men, wear a tie. Even if your hearing is virtual, dress as you would for the actual courtroom. Many judges have expressed disapproval of how some lawyers dress for virtual court appearances. Hoodies, sweatshirts, and even collared dress shirts (without a jacket and tie) are not appropriate for virtual court appearances. Judges do not take the bench wearing Tommy Bahama. They expect the same respect for the judicial process from attorneys. You must never dress in a way that might be perceived as disrespectful of the court, whether you are appearing virtually or in person.

If you appear in court in person, be sure your suit is clean and pressed. You will notice other attorneys showing up in rumpled clothing that sometimes does not even match. Don't be them. You need not dress in very expensive attire, but dress like you have your act together. Guys, learn how to tie a necktie. A poorly tied tie will make you look unsophisticated.

Bring your notes and papers in a briefcase or organized neatly in a binder or folder. Do not bring your whole case file or a mass of seemingly random notes and documents. Bring only what you are likely to need: the motion and opposition papers (and an extra copy of your papers for the court in case they are missing from the court's file), copies of key case authority, copies of any pleadings or deposition excerpts you might need, and your outline of your argument. Some lawyers prefer to bring a computer or tablet instead of paper copies. If you do so, be sure your battery is fully charged and that you will not have to spend time booting up your device. The court will not wait for you. Also, do not depend on the court providing a Wi-Fi signal. New or recently renovated courthouses are more tech savvy, but many courthouses are still living in the 20th century where technology is concerned. Unless you are certain that your technology will work flawlessly for you, bring paper copies, at least as a backup.

Be Nice to the Clerk

You might think the judge runs the courtroom, but more often it's the courtroom deputy clerk. Judges come and go among courtrooms, but the courtroom deputy clerk is usually a permanent fixture, protected by civil service laws and probably a union too. The clerk manages the calendar and the document flow in the courtroom. Many clerks are genuinely nice people. Some have more challenging personalities. If you encounter one of the latter, don't take it personally. A courtroom deputy clerk might have to check in 40 or more attorneys before a court session starts, so they ordinarily don't have time to be chatty. When court is in session, they are busy assisting the judge to move through the calendar. When court is not in session, they usually are busy processing documents from the day's calendar and all of the new documents coming into the courtroom that day, so they might not pick up the phone on your first call. Regardless of the clerk's demeanor, treat them with respect and consideration. If you do, they generally will help you when they can. If you don't, you might find that the judge did not receive your reply brief or that your hearing fell off the calendar.

Be Prepared for Your Hearing

Your first court hearing is likely to be either a case management conference or a motion hearing such as a motion to dismiss or a motion to compel discovery.

Case management conferences are usually routine. Their primary purpose is to assign a trial date and other key dates such as the discovery cutoff, expert witness disclosure deadline, settlement conference, and so on. In most federal courts, you will have "met and conferred" with your opposing counsel before the case management conference to propose a schedule of dates to the court, and the court will usually accept the proposed dates if they are reasonable. In some courts you will not see the judge for a case management conference; the courtroom deputy clerk assigns the dates. In about 50 percent of cases, the setting of dates is all that occurs during the case management conference. The only preparation you will need in such an event is familiarity with the calendar of the partner(s) who will try the case. You will want to be sure you will not be assigned a trial date when the lead trial counsel is already scheduled for another trial or has plans to be away on vacation. Therefore, you should have your assistant contact the courtroom deputy clerk to learn when the court is currently setting trial dates, and then check with the trial partner(s) or their assistants regarding their calendars during that same time frame.

Then there's the other 50 percent of cases. In those cases, the judge engages counsel on both sides in a discussion of the case to a greater or lesser extent. What are the plaintiff's allegations? What are the defendant's key defenses? Will either side move for summary judgment? Are there any discovery issues that need to be addressed in advance? Will there be experts? How many trial days do you anticipate needing? Have the parties discussed settlement? Will the parties attend private mediation, or will a settlement conference with the court be required? Typically, the judge will address these questions to counsel from the bench, but sometimes counsel will be called to meet with the judge in chambers.

Unless you are absolutely certain that your case is *not* one of these 50 percent, you must be prepared for the possibility that the judge will want to have a conversation with you about your case. Therefore, know the answers to all of the preceding questions before you go to the hearing. You do not want to be standing before the judge, especially in open court, saying, "I don't know that much detail about the case, Your Honor; the partner just sent me here to get a trial date." The reaction from the judge will range from disappointed eye-rolling to issuance of sanctions with an order that the lead trial partner appear in court for a continued case management conference. Returning from court to inform the partner that your first case management conference was a "loss" is not the optimal path toward star associate status.

If you will be arguing a contested motion, your preparation will obviously be different. During your argument, do not plan simply to repeat what you wrote in your briefs. The judge is likely to cut you off and say, "Counsel, I've read your briefs. Is there anything else?" You will have limited time to argue most motions, so choose a key point or two to address with the court. If you are the moving party, state briefly why you should win and why your opponent has not shown the contrary. If you are the opposing party, state briefly why the motion should be denied and why the moving party's arguments fail. As the opposing party, you might also take advantage of your opportunity to address a point in your opponent's reply brief that you were not able to address previously.

Some courts will issue a tentative ruling on a motion in advance of the hearing. If both parties agree, the tentative ruling will become the final ruling of the court. If either party wants to argue the motion, they must notify the court clerk by a specified deadline. If the tentative ruling is against you, focus your argument on where you will contend that the ruling is mistaken as you attempt to convince the court to change its ruling. Look especially for appellate court authority contrary to the court's tentative ruling. Courts do change tentative rulings, so don't give up just yet.

If the tentative ruling is in your favor, don't pop the cork on the champagne yet, either. As the judge said in one of my cases, "Some tentatives are more tentative than others." In that case, a major motion was scheduled to be heard on July 5. The tentative ruling, which I received on July 3, was in my favor. I did not cancel my plans to spend July 4 preparing for the hearing to go to a picnic and watch fireworks, though. I spent July 4 in the office, reviewing the important case law and outlining the argument I would present orally the next day in case it became necessary. It became necessary. After announcing that his tentative ruling was still tentative, the judge heard an hour and a half of oral argument on the motion. We still won, but had I assumed we had won based on the tentative ruling and spent July 4 relaxing instead of preparing, it would have been a disaster.

When you prepare to argue a motion, review the supporting and opposing briefs, but do not simply remind yourself of the arguments in your favor. Instead, focus on your opponent's brief(s) and think about how you will address their strongest arguments at the hearing, even if those arguments have been addressed in the briefing. Outline your oral presentation around responding to those arguments, not merely repeating your own.

If there is case law that is potentially determinative of the motion, print the cases and highlight the important language. If the court seems unsure of, or unfamiliar with, the case law on point, you will want to be able to pick up the case and read an excerpt from it. Read the whole case as you prepare, however. Be sure that the result in the case is the same result you seek from the court in your case. Judges love to say, "Well, counsel, I hear what you are saying, but didn't the *Gersten* court decide the case the other way?" If that is the situation, you must be prepared to argue why the language in the case upon which you rely is still dispositive even though the case was decided the other way. Usually, you can make the argument by showing how the facts in the two cases differ.

The same goes for any statutes or regulations upon which you are relying. If you are arguing that the plaintiff's complaint should be dismissed on statute of limitations grounds, have the applicable statute of limitations before you. If there is a statute that requires the plaintiff to exhaust her internal remedies before filing a lawsuit and she failed to do so, have that statute handy in case the court has questions about what it says.

Also as you prepare, highlight any excerpts of the pleadings, interrogatory responses, or deposition transcripts that might support your motion or opposition. If you are moving to compel further responses to interrogatories, your opponent's previous responses will be relevant, so have them highlighted and at your fingertips at oral argument. If your opponent's client testified in a deposition that she kept a personal diary listing each incident of her manager's harassment of her or her coworkers but in her responses to your document requests she said no diary exists, have the deposition testimony highlighted and ready to read to the court if necessary.

Throughout your preparation for oral argument, do not be confident that your arguments are the better ones and that you will prevail. Rather, focus on your opponent's arguments and how you will respond if the court seems to be leaning in the direction of your opponent or asks for further support for your position. Only when you are satisfied that you can persuasively address each of your opponent's key points, as well as your own principal arguments, will your preparation be complete.

Show Respect for the Court

This sounds like an obvious point, but inexperienced lawyers often fail to do it, albeit usually unwittingly.

First, show up on time. Give yourself plenty of time to get to the courthouse and through the security line. The line can be long if it's at the start of a day when a new group of jurors has been summoned. If you are driving to the courthouse for a morning hearing, account for rush-hour traffic. Regardless of the hearing time, account for your need to find parking, which might be a few blocks away from the courthouse. Bring some cash, too, because courthouse-area parking can be expensive and some parking vendors do not accept credit cards.

Second, bring your business cards with you. When the clerk checks you in for the hearing, he or she might ask you for a business card or two; typically the clerk keeps one and gives one to the court reporter.[11] You do not want to be one of those attorneys standing in front of the clerk writing your name and contact information on scraps of paper.

Third, there are rules and customs for where you stand in the courtroom. Generally, the plaintiff's attorney stands at the counsel table closest to the jury box, and the defense attorney stands at the other counsel table. Sometimes for motions practice, however, the court will direct that counsel for the moving party stand closest to the jury box and counsel for the responding party stand at the other table. Usually, when this is the court's preference, there are small signs that say "Moving Party" and "Responding Party" on the tables. If you are unsure of where you should stand, ask the courtroom deputy clerk or the marshal or bailiff before the court session begins.

Fourth, unless the court indicates otherwise, always stand when you address the court. In federal court this will almost always be the rule. Practice in state courts varies, but when in doubt, stand. If there is a lectern placed between the counsel tables, that is a good sign that the court expects counsel to stand at the lectern when addressing the court. Again, if you are unclear where you should stand, ask the clerk, marshal, or bailiff.

---

11. Due to budget constraints, some state courts have stopped providing court reporters for civil nonevidentiary hearings. In those courts, if you want a court reporter, you will have to arrange for one to appear at your hearing at your client's expense. If there is any chance your client might want to appeal the court's ruling on your motion, you will need an official transcript of the hearing. Consult with your supervising partner regarding the need for a court reporter, and if one is needed, give your assistant a few days' advance notice to make arrangements.

Fifth, you must never "traverse the well," meaning that you must not walk in the area between the counsel tables and the judge's bench while court is in session. This is a custom that goes back centuries to a time when lawyers and litigants brought their swords to court and it was necessary to keep them at least a sword's distance away from the judge for the judge's safety. Today, even though courthouse security will not allow you to bring your sword into the courthouse, staying out of the well of the courtroom is still considered a sign of respect for the court, and many judges will call you out if you should fail to do so. If the judge asks counsel to approach the bench for a sidebar conference, therefore, always walk around the back of the counsel tables, not in front of them, as you walk toward the bench.

Sixth, never hand a document directly to the judge. The judge might ask you for a copy of the case upon which you are relying, relevant deposition testimony, or a responsive pleading that you filed that is missing from the court's file. If this happens, hand the document to the marshal or bailiff to hand to the judge. If there is no marshal or bailiff in court, ask the judge if you may approach the clerk and hand the document to him or her.

Seventh, if you are examining a witness and you need to hand the witness a document or focus his or her attention on a particular passage, always ask the court if you may approach the witness each time before you do so. Again, be careful to walk around the back of the counsel tables and not in front of them as you walk toward the witness.

In addressing the court, always refer to the judge as "Your Honor." More experienced practitioners might get away with addressing the judge as "Judge," but you should not do so. Also, never refer to the judge as "sir" or "ma'am." Always respond with "yes, Your Honor" or "no, Your Honor." Moreover, never express familiarity with the judge in the courtroom, even though you clerked for the judge or you serve with the judge on a bar committee. Your doing so might make the judge seem less than impartial to your opponent, and that will be a big problem for the judge.

When you introduce yourself to the court at the start of your presentation, state your full name and the name of your law firm. The judge will likely never have heard of you, but she probably has heard of your law firm, and your affiliation with your firm will (hopefully) help you to establish credibility with the court. The only time you might want to skip announcing your firm affiliation is if you are an associate with a large law firm and you are appearing in a small-town courtroom.

During your argument, never interrupt the judge. If the judge interrupts you, stop talking and listen to the judge's statement or question. The judge does not mean to be rude, but most courts have crowded motion calendars, and they have to use their time very efficiently. If a judge asks you a question, answer it. The question indicates that the court is still undecided and wants to hear your response before deciding. Answering the court's question well can be the most important thing you do during your argument. This is why you must be thoroughly prepared to answer questions the judge might ask you.

Never lie to the court. If you do not know the answer to the court's question, say so. Do not attempt to make up an answer. The judge will know you are faking it because you will not be the first attorney to have tried. Also, if the court asks a factual question, such as if your client was served or if your client failed to appear for a deposition, give a factual and truthful answer. If you attempt to equivocate or to change the subject, you will lose credibility with the court. Tell the truth, even if it's not pretty.

Most of the time during oral argument, one attorney or the other will be addressing the court in an orderly fashion. If the judge asks a question of your opponent, never interrupt your opponent's answer or interject yourself into the dialogue between the judge and your opponent. Even if your opponent is telling a blatant lie, wait for your opponent to finish and then ask if you may address the court on that issue. If the court allows you to do so, address the lack of accuracy of your opponent's answer and provide proof for your position if you can. Do not attack your opponent personally by calling him or her a "liar" or "disingenuous."[12] Judges hate ad hominem attacks between lawyers. Most judges got to be judges by getting along with their fellow members of the bar, and they expect you to do so as well.

Finally, don't snatch defeat from the jaws of victory. Know when to stop. An important skill for a lawyer is knowing how to read a room, and when you are reading a courtroom without a jury, the judge is the only person you will read. If the judge seems satisfied with your presentation and skeptical of your opponent's, *sit down*. If you continue arguing, you might say something to cause the court to reconsider.

No matter how well prepared you are, and no matter how much the controlling law supports your position, you still might not win. Courts hate to be reversed, so they are reluctant to grant a motion to dismiss a case before the evidence is developed. They would much prefer to consider the merits on a motion for summary judgment after the parties have conducted discovery and the issues are better developed. Even if a court grants your motion to dismiss, it might also give the plaintiff leave to amend the complaint to try again to state a claim. These are not reasons not to file a motion to dismiss; there may be strategic reasons to do so. Just keep in mind if you lose that the odds were not in your favor.

Where discovery motions are concerned, often courts are guided more by the equities than by a strict application of the law. You might have done everything right in your case and your opponent might have done everything wrong, but the court might be unwilling to come down hard on the other side. I once had a case where the plaintiff failed to show up for his deposition three successive times, with opposing counsel (two solo practitioners) notifying us a day or two beforehand each time that they essentially were too busy to attend the deposition. After the third time, I lost patience with them and filed a motion to compel the plaintiff's deposition with a request for sanctions. Instead of ordering

12. This is a fancy courtroom term for "liar."

the plaintiff to appear for deposition, the court admonished me for wasting its time and not working out the problem with opposing counsel. The court was not willing to punish opposing counsel and their client because counsel were too busy to appear for my deposition. Sometimes that happens. Sometimes courts simply reach the wrong decision, but in most discovery disputes courts seek to do what they perceive as the right thing for the parties, not necessarily for the lawyers.

Once the court has announced its ruling, do not attempt to continue arguing with the judge. You will not change the court's mind at that point. You will only impress the judge with your lack of professionalism. Accept the result and thank the court. If the court's ruling amounts to a significant injustice, your client may appeal.

If you were thoroughly prepared for your hearing as suggested in this chapter, yet you were still unsuccessful, you will not have failed and you will not be judged negatively for it. You got valuable experience on your feet in a courtroom by yourself, and that's where stellar legal careers begin. No litigator wins every motion or hearing. What matters is that you gave it your absolute best.

Treat Your Opponent with Respect and Professionalism

Showing respect for your opponent goes beyond merely not attacking them personally during oral argument. There is a tendency among some lawyers toward viewing the opposing party as a lower form of life undeserving of common courtesy or consideration and viewing their lawyer as not much better. This is a mistake. Regardless of the character of the opposing party in your case, your opposing counsel is simply doing his or her job. It is a hallowed principle in our legal system that every litigant has the right to legal counsel. Most lawyers do not have the luxury of picking their clients and cases. A defendant accused of the most grievous misconduct still has the right to counsel, as does a plaintiff pursuing the most frivolous of claims. The litigants might behave badly during the case, too. They might lie. They might destroy evidence. They might fail to show up for their deposition. They might verbally attack your client personally and not use the King's English in doing so. It happens in litigation.

It is in your and your client's best interest that you try to get along with your opposing counsel in a case, however, no matter how badly behaved their client. Lawyers are professionals and are considered officers of the court. This means that you are expected to rise above the acrimony and emotion in a case and move the case toward a resolution without becoming mired in personal grievances with opposing counsel. I was taught this lesson when I was a combative junior lawyer and the representative of an important client told me he was tired of paying legal bills resulting from my disputes with opposing counsel. He told me to find a way to get along with opposing counsel or he would find a new lawyer. It was extremely valuable advice, and it changed my approach toward practicing law.

Undoubtedly you will encounter lawyers in litigation who are belligerent, uncooperative, and eager to obtain any advantage using sharp practices. If you engage with them in that game, though, you will have lost an early round. Your case will be much more difficult to manage and much more expensive for your client than it otherwise might have been.

The far better option is to maintain a consistent approach of professionalism and collegiality with opposing counsel from the beginning of a case until its conclusion, regardless of whether it is reciprocated. Introduce yourself at the beginning of a case with a phone call or at least an email. If you appear in person at a case management conference or motion hearing, shake hands with your opponent and introduce yourself at the beginning or end of the proceeding. Avoid writing long, accusatory screeds to opposing counsel regarding perceived defects in their clients' discovery responses. Rather, pick up the phone and try to resolve the issues in a conversation. You might not be completely successful, but you will probably be able to narrow the issues a bit for further negotiations. If a motion to compel discovery becomes necessary, do not automatically seek sanctions against your opponent unless their client has completely failed to appear or respond. Most courts will not award sanctions in discovery disputes if the parties appear to be acting in good faith and have reached a genuine impasse. Your pursuing sanctions nonetheless can poison an otherwise decent working relationship with opposing counsel or exacerbate an already difficult relationship. Even when opposing counsel seeks sanctions in a routine discovery dispute, I typically do not ask for sanctions in return. Instead, I state in my brief that it is not my practice to seek sanctions with respect to motions of this type.[13]

Continue your approach of professionalism when you take or defend depositions. Consult with your opponent about available dates before scheduling depositions.[14] Do not engage in arguments with opposing counsel on the record of a deposition. Your opponent might try to draw you into such an argument, but don't take the bait. Rather, state simply that you will not engage in argument with counsel on the record. Repeat that statement as many times as counsel attempts to argue with you. Eventually, your opponent will become tired of trying to argue with you on the record, and the deposition will go more smoothly.

In negotiating resolution of issues in the litigation or a settlement of the case, be a lawyer of your word. Be sure you can back up any representations you make, then when you make the representation, stand by it. Do not make a representation and renege on it. This means that you must have authority from your client to make or accept a settlement offer, to commit the client to appear for a deposition or produce requested documents, or to deliver a

13. You might need to consult with your client regarding the decision not to pursue sanctions. Check with your supervising partner.

14. In some jurisdictions, it is important for the defendant to notice the plaintiff's deposition first in order to establish priority in the taking of depositions. If you must unilaterally schedule a deposition, notify opposing counsel that you will be flexible with the date should they have a scheduling conflict.

settlement payment by a specific deadline. Do not merely assume that you do, because if your client is not on board, your credibility will be seriously undermined.

When your opposing counsel requests an extension of a deadline, agree to it unless doing so will prejudice your client's interests in the case. Most of the time it will not. Karma is real in litigation as in most other aspects of life. Lawyers are people, and sometimes life gets messy. Your courtesy and consideration will be returned, maybe not in the same case, but it will be returned.[15]

For example, I had a case in which we served initial written discovery on opposing counsel but never heard back from them. We contacted them after their deadline to respond had passed, and they responded that a staff person had mishandled the incoming discovery and it was never calendared. My associate wanted to assert that opposing counsel had waived all objections and to demand immediate answers. We would have been justified in doing so, but I didn't think it was the best option under the circumstances. Instead, we told opposing counsel to consider that day as the date they received our discovery requests and to respond in 30 days. They were very grateful, and our concession set the tone for good relations with opposing counsel for the rest of the case, yet we did not have to give up anything meaningful. It was still early in the case, so another 30 days made no difference. Moreover, most courts would have granted relief to opposing counsel under the circumstances because courts are reluctant to penalize clients for the mistakes of their lawyers. By agreeing to reset opposing counsel's deadline for responding to our discovery, the only thing we lost was the opportunity to send our client a bill for litigating opposing counsel's likely successful motion for relief. Our client was good with that.

---

15. On occasion, your firm might be directed by a client to take a very aggressive approach toward the opposite party and their counsel. This sometimes occurs where a client is dealing with a serial plaintiff or with a competitor that it suspects of stealing its trade secrets. Those occasions are somewhat rare, but if you are working on such a case, take your cues from the supervising partner regarding whether to agree to opposing counsel's requests for deadline extensions.

Karma caught up to us a few months later. We had been waiting for weeks for an open courtroom to start a long-delayed trial. We finally found one, and the judge ordered us to appear in court in two hours. On our drive to the courthouse, we contacted our expert witnesses to inform them that the trial would be starting. We learned that one of our experts was in intensive care with a serious case of pneumonia and would not be able to testify anytime soon. When we arrived in court, we reported this new development to the court and opposing counsel. Opposing counsel and the court were amenable to delaying the start of trial for about a month so we could determine if our expert would recover in time to testify or locate a new expert and produce him for deposition. You should never believe, therefore, no matter how prepared or well organized you are, that you will never need the indulgence of the court or opposing counsel. Be accommodating of real-life issues when you are able to do so, and it will come back to you.

At the end of a case, win, lose, or settle, accept the outcome graciously. If you lose, congratulate your opponents. If you win, compliment your opponents on their efforts. If you settle, include in your letter transmitting the settlement check, or your email sending the executed settlement agreement, an expression of appreciation of your opponents' professionalism. You might well face the same opposing counsel again in another case. Better yet, they might refer clients to you or serve as a resource if you need to refer a client to an attorney in their practice area. Many times I have received referrals from, and sent referrals to, previous opposing counsel. Maintaining good relationships with opposing counsel is an important aspect of building your network.

9
If You Make a Mistake

You screwed up.

It Happens

OK, so you made a mistake. Most associates do at one time or another. Will this be the end of your career? Probably not, depending on what happened and how you handle it moving forward.

If you simply made a mistake, you should be OK. Errors by junior lawyers include missing a key case or statute while doing research, missing a court deadline for a filing, making procedural errors in filing a motion or other document, missing a key piece of evidence because the client failed to provide it and you failed to ask for it, missing a client's time-sensitive email, or giving erroneous advice to a client. These mistakes are not to be wished for, but they happen, unfortunately.

Don't Hide It

The most important thing to do when you make a mistake is to admit it and report it. Report it promptly to your supervising partner, your mentor, or your office managing partner. Reporting it will be difficult and embarrassing, but you must do so. The sooner you report it, the sooner you and your firm can correct the situation.

It's always better for you to bring your mistake to the attention of firm management than for someone else (a partner, opposing counsel, the client, or the court) to do so. The worst thing you can do is try to hide your mistake. If you do, your relatively minor error will have a cascading effect and become a much larger problem. Also, if you try to hide your mistake, your firm will view it not only as an error on your part but also as an integrity issue, and the latter can be much more damaging to your career. "It's not the crime, it's the cover-up," as they say.

Most minor mistakes have fixes. If you have made an effort to maintain a good relationship with opposing counsel, they are not as likely to attempt to capitalize on your error than if your relationship with them is acrimonious. The courts have dealt with minor attorney errors before, moreover. Most courts will not punish a client for their lawyer's error. Your firm might have to pay some of your opponent's attorneys' fees or costs as a sanction, but these kinds of problems can be remedied. You might not win the Associate of the Year award this year as the result of your error, but if you promptly take responsibility for it and continue to deliver consistently strong performance, your mistake should not hold you back over the long term.

Apologize

Many attorneys are afraid to apologize for a mistake, for fear of showing weakness or admitting culpability. They might apologize in a superficial fashion when they feel they must, but genuine apologies, especially to courts, are somewhat rare. I know this because I have seen how judges are taken aback when it occurs. I have apologized twice to judges in my career. Both times it resulted in turning around what otherwise likely would have been a negative and unpleasant outcome.

One of those instances occurred when I was an associate. My firm assigned me to handle a small lawsuit between two local businesses in a suburban county outside of Atlanta. I filed a motion for summary judgment, and my opposing counsel raised an argument in opposition that I had not anticipated. I researched the law behind his argument and found a case directly on point that refuted his argument. On facts very similar to mine, the appellate court upheld the trial court's grant of summary judgment for the party in the same position as my client. I made that case the centerpiece of my reply brief.

The night before the argument on my motion I could not sleep, however. The case I found seemed almost too good to be true, and I could not understand why my opponent, a litigator with decades more experience than me, relied on an argument that was so squarely rejected by the court of appeals. Then it occurred to me that in my rush to get my reply brief filed, I had not Shepardized the case. Back then, Shepardizing required looking in a series of books and paperback supplements to ensure a case was still good law. So I got dressed at 3 a.m. and drove downtown to the office. I Shepardized the case and found that it had been reversed by the state supreme court. I felt like an enormous idiot.

When I appeared in court later that morning, I started my presentation with an apology to the court and opposing counsel for citing a case that I had not Shepardized. The judge graciously accepted my apology, as did my opponent. There were no snarky comments from my opponent about the "big firm downtown lawyer" making such an obvious error and no sanctions from the court. The judge said he appreciated my candor and professionalism in accepting responsibility. I lost my motion, as it was defeated by the case I failed to find in Shepard's, but the day could have ended much worse.

The other instance occurred more recently. An associate in my office had attempted to remove a case to federal court. I will spare the details about what went wrong, but the case was not removable. The federal judge issued an order to show cause, and I thought having the associate appear for the hearing and try to explain what happened was not a good idea. I went to court instead and apologized on behalf of my law firm. I told the judge I was unaware of the removal attempt when it occurred, but I accepted responsibility for it as managing partner of the office. The judge's demeanor changed instantly. His dark frown turned into a broad smile. He said no one had ever come to his court to apologize like that before. He said he had considered imposing Rule 11 sanctions, but my apology changed his mind, and he concluded the matter by paying my firm a nice compliment.

Don't expect your office managing partner to go to court to apologize for you when you make a mistake. I cite these examples only to show that an apology to the court for even the dumbest of mistakes can turn the situation around for you. If (and probably when) you make a mistake, own it. Bring it to the attention of your firm and apologize to all who were affected by it, including the court. A sincere apology can go a long way.

If You Need Help

By "help" here I mean attention from a health care professional. Errors sometimes occur, but if you find yourself repeatedly missing deadlines or producing work product containing mistakes, you must take a good look at yourself and ask if something more serious is going wrong. Even if you do not make errors, if you find yourself paralyzed by anxiety sometimes or you are unable to get out of bed some mornings, you might be affected by something more serious than just nerves or a bad mood.

Law practice is a high-stress profession. It is even more stressful as you are still learning and finding your way. Most lawyers like to believe they are resilient enough to handle the stress, but that's not always the case. Lawyers, like other professionals, are susceptible to depression, anxiety, and other mental health challenges. This can be especially true if you moved to a new city to start your law career and you no longer have your former support system consisting of family and old friends close by, if you had a recent breakup with a significant other, or if you have had mental health episodes earlier in life.

Some lawyers think that admitting they need mental health treatment will ruin their career. Not so. Generations ago that might have been the case, but given today's understanding of mental illness and laws protecting those with mental disabilities, it is much more accepted that talented attorneys might experience mental illness during their careers. Like most challenges you will experience as a lawyer, how you handle a mental health issue will determine whether it will damage your career over the long term. If you seek help promptly, you will likely minimize its effect. If you ignore it until it becomes a crisis manifest in erratic behavior, serious self-harm, or drug or alcohol abuse, it could have a much greater impact on your future.

Your firm's health plan almost certainly covers mental health treatment, and the fact that you are seeing a mental health professional must be held in the strictest confidence under current medical privacy laws. Current law requires that mental health treatment be accorded the same level of confidentiality as other types of medical treatment. You should not worry that your being treated for mental illness will be broadcast across the firm. If you need to take time off work to attend sessions with a counselor or a therapist, you need not be specific about the treatment you are receiving. Simply state that you must attend a medical appointment, if you need to give a reason for your absence at all.

The type of mental health treatment you receive will depend on the type and severity of your condition. You might need to see a psychiatrist for medication and a psychologist or counselor for psychotherapy sessions. Consider seeing a psychiatrist who can assess your situation and prescribe a treatment plan. If the treatment plan includes counseling or therapy, the psychiatrist will likely provide a referral. You can locate a psychiatrist in your health plan's directory of physicians. If you have a regular physician whom you see for an annual checkup and routine medical issues, you might start with a visit to him or her to describe your situation. Today's primary care physicians are trained to screen for mental health conditions and to help direct their patients to appropriate treatment.

You must take care of yourself if you are going to excel in the practice of law. An important part of that self-care is recognizing when you need professional help and obtaining it. Just as you would seek medical attention if you had appendicitis or diabetes, you must seek the appropriate help if you have a mental health disorder. Your future in the law might depend on it.

10

Business Development

You might be thinking, "I just became a lawyer! How can I develop business?" or "Isn't business development what the firm's rainmakers do? Or is it the marketing department?" Relax. You are not expected to bring clients to the firm in your first few years of practice. This is because your corner coffee house, veterinarian, or dry cleaner, who might actually hire you, does not need the firm's firepower and cannot afford it in any event. This is not to say, however, that you should not start thinking about business development at the very outset of your career.

Every lawyer in private practice must think about business development every day, because eventually you will be expected to develop enough client business to keep yourself and other lawyers at the firm busy. Ultimately, your compensation and security in a law firm will be based on how much revenue you bring into the firm. If you do not develop your own clients eventually, you probably won't become a partner, and you will not have much control over your own destiny. As soon as there is a downturn in the legal industry, and downturns always occur, you might well be laid off.

The problem with many lawyers is that they do not begin to think about business development until they are within a year or two of partnership eligibility. By then it's usually too late. They have to try to learn skills that should have been honed earlier in their careers, and it can be difficult to get started at such a late date. It is especially difficult for such lawyers to compete with colleagues who have been working on business development for several years already.

Business development does not require some mystical quality that only "rainmakers" have. It mostly involves building your network, establishing genuine relationships with prospective clients, and then, when you get your opportunity, providing consistently excellent client service. It does not just happen, though, and it takes more than just being a good lawyer. There are many excellent lawyers in law firms who have no clients of their own. Don't be them. In this chapter we'll examine how you can excel at business development even in your early years as a lawyer.

Internal and External Marketplaces

When they think about business development, many lawyers focus only on the *external* marketplace, the place where lawyers must go to find new clients and bring them into the firm. Eventually you too will focus your efforts on the external marketplace, but as you get started, your firm's *internal* marketplace will provide a fertile environment in which you can hone your business development skills. Your firm's internal marketplace consists of two elements: the partners in your firm and your firm's existing clients.

As a new associate, you are competing in your firm's internal marketplace. You are competing for work assignments, and for the best work assignments. The partners in your firm are your clients now. Most of them have the ability to select among several associates to handle work for their clients, just as external clients have their pick of law firms. Like external clients, they will want to work with associates who are responsive and able to deliver a superior work product in a timely and efficient fashion. As you compete for the best work assignments in your firm, therefore, you will be developing the same skills and talents necessary to compete successfully for clients outside of the firm. You will learn how to be highly responsive to partners when they need your help. You will learn how to identify and meet a partner's work style and preferences. You will learn how to be proactive, to anticipate what needs to be done instead of waiting to be told. You will learn how to develop excellent writing and communication skills so that the legal work you perform will be understood by your audience. You will learn how to see clients' legal problems as practical business problems to be solved expeditiously. You will learn how to work efficiently and economically so that your time is not written off and a client will pay for it. You might think you are just becoming a better associate as you master these skills, but in reality you are becoming a better business developer as well. The service you provide to the partners in your firm will be a template for the service that you will provide to the firm's clients.

Your firm's existing clients are the second element of your internal marketplace. As an associate you will get practice providing the best possible service to these clients, using the same skills you developed in serving the firm's partners. If your excellent service for these clients causes them to send even more business to your firm, that will be a big win for you. Most law firms prefer to obtain more business from existing clients than to have to wrest new clients away from competitors.

If you find yourself working consistently for a particular client of the firm, try to develop a good relationship with the client representative. Your goal is to move the client representative with whom you work from "I am going to send this new matter to Law Firm X because it is within their area of practice and we have worked with them before" to "I'm going to send this new matter to Lawyer Y because I enjoy working with her." You will not establish that kind of relationship quickly, especially as a junior associate. It will take time and is an investment, and it will not always work. The two of you simply might not connect well. Or you might invest a year or more in developing a relationship with a client representative only to have him change jobs and move to a new company firmly committed to using another law firm. When it does work, however, you will establish a strong and ongoing working relationship with the client.

How do you establish such a relationship? By doing all of the things we have covered in this book *plus* getting to know the client representative as a person. This might occur initially over lunch, during a client site visit, or at a client seminar presented by your firm. The relationship can be developed further by finding things in common with the client representative during conversations you will have about the matters you are working on for the client. Look for cues during those conversations to get to know the client representative better. Perhaps you will discover that you lived in the same area growing up, or you both play the same musical instrument, or you are both fans of wine from a particular region, or you both have children who are of similar age or who are involved in the same activities. Maybe the client representative is going on vacation to a place you visited last year, and you can recommend a restaurant or activity there. Take note of significant events in the client representative's life such as the birth of a child, a move to a new home, or the taking of an overseas vacation and inquire about those events. Don't intrude into sensitive personal issues, but show a genuine interest in the person's life outside of work. Keep the relationship strictly professional, but make it comfortable for the client representative to interact and work with you, and the relationship is likely to last and result in the client representative's seeking you out for additional assignments in the future.

When working for an existing client of the firm, therefore, don't think of it as simply completing assignments, handling cases, or billing hours. Consider it an opportunity to further hone your client service skills. Your understanding that you are not just providing legal services, that you are in the client service business too, will make you that much more successful when it's time for you to develop clients in your firm's external marketplace.

Build Your Network in Your Firm

One important way to elevate your visibility in your firm's internal marketplace is to build your network inside your firm. Especially if your firm has multiple offices, you will want to get to know as many partners and associates in those other offices as you can. Your goal should be for those lawyers to reach out to you when they have a need for a lawyer in your city and in your area of specialization. Most corporate clients today prefer that local lawyers handle local matters unless the matter is highly specialized, which is why so many former regional law firms have become national firms. When a partner in the Boston office receives a call from a client with a new case in Denver and you are in the Denver office, you want that Boston partner to think of you. How can you accomplish this?

Many firms have attorney retreats. They present excellent opportunities to meet lawyers in other offices, and you should attend every one of them and engage with other lawyers as much as you can. Do not just stick around the other lawyers from your office when you are there. Get out of your comfort zone. Approach lawyers from other offices and introduce yourself. Participate in activities and team-building events. Unless seats are assigned, make it a point to sit with strangers during meals and engage them in conversation. Do the same at cocktail parties. Follow up after the retreat with the attorneys you met, especially those with whom you found a connection. Send an email or a LinkedIn invitation. Simply say you enjoyed meeting them at dinner, at a reception, or while participating in a particular activity and that you hope to stay in touch.

Another way to expand your network inside your firm is to serve on a firmwide committee or task force. Most larger law firms frequently have these committees and task forces working on one thing or another. Some might address internal issues such as diversity and inclusion, associate morale and retention, or technology. Others might address external issues such as a new law or a new exigency facing the firm's clients. During the COVID pandemic, my firm created numerous attorney task forces to develop pandemic-related content for clients and to provide special services for clients such as assisting them in qualifying as essential critical infrastructure or obtaining Paycheck Protection Program (PPP) loans. Several ambitious associates volunteered for these task forces, and a few of them gained high visibility in the firm as a result. They developed firmwide reputations for coming up with creative solutions for clients and for being available 24/7 during a time of nonstop client need. They are partners now and future leaders in the firm.

Fortunately, worldwide pandemics are not frequent occurrences, but many law firms continue to offer opportunities for lawyers, including associates, to become involved in firmwide committees and initiatives. If your firm offers such an opportunity, go for it. You will meet partners and associates from other offices to help build your network, and you will develop an expertise that might cause others in the firm to seek you out, making you valuable to the firm beyond just in your own office.

Another way to get to know lawyers in another office is to stop by the firm's office in a city you are visiting. You might be in town for a wedding or to see your sister's new baby. Even though it's a personal trip, you should not shut off your thinking about business development. Most firms encourage office visits by attorneys from other offices, but know your firm's policy or protocol. Don't just show up without warning. Reach out to a partner or associate in that office with whom you worked on a firmwide task force or whom you met at the last attorney retreat. If you don't know anyone in the office, ask your mentor or your office's managing partner to make an introduction to someone. Contact that lawyer and ask if he or she is available for coffee or lunch when you visit. Before or after such a meeting, the lawyer will likely offer you a tour around the office and introductions to other attorneys, particularly those in your practice area.

Yet another way to build your network within your firm is to respond promptly when a lawyer in another office sends an email firmwide or to your office asking a question about a topic within your expertise. When the email arrives asking, "What is the statute of limitations for a breach of oral contract claim in Colorado?," if you can provide the correct answer, do so promptly. The attorney who posed the question will remember you favorably for your fast and helpful response.[16]

Finally, if you happen to be assigned to perform work for a lawyer in another office, produce a result that is timely, excellent, and responsive to the scope of the assignment. Know when the lawyer needs your response and deliver it on time. From the standpoint of a partner who often sends work to lawyers in other offices, I will tell you there are two things that I find extremely annoying. One is when the lawyer to whom I assigned the work does not respond for days. If I say on Wednesday that I need for you to review a draft sales commission agreement that the client must have by Friday, and Friday afternoon arrives and I have heard nothing from you, that's not good. If you receive such an assignment, you should acknowledge it and communicate with the assigning partner regarding your ability to meet the deadline. I know you're busy, but meeting the deadline on this assignment from a partner in another office will win you a new ally in that office.

The other mistake that lawyers often make when performing an assignment from a lawyer in another office is that they go too far beyond the scope of the assignment. If I send you a draft sales commission agreement to review for compliance with your state's law, *I do not want you to rewrite the agreement!* I only need for you to tell me where it is not compliant or to redline a few suggested changes to make it compliant. Don't send me a different document and tell me, "This is how we write sales commission agreements here." I do not want something that departs from my template because the client uses that template in several other jurisdictions. Moreover, you have billed three hours of time for a task that should have taken less than an hour. If this is you, you will certainly make a name for yourself in the firm, but it will not be in a manner that is helpful toward enhancing your reputation as a go-to resource

16. Don't "reply all," however. The entire law firm need not receive your answer, and lawyers in the firm who have never heard of you will identify you as either being inconsiderate or trying too hard to impress others as they read your email that has no relevance to them whatsoever.

in your office. If you are at all unsure what a lawyer in another office expects or how long your work should take, get clarification before you start working.

Develop Genuine Relationships Outside of the Firm

In addition to performing well in the firm's internal marketplace, junior associates also should be working on business development in the firm's external marketplace. I do not mean you should be out pounding the pavement looking for clients. Rather, you should focus on building genuine relationships with people who might become clients or referral sources someday down the road.

By *genuine* relationships I mean that you take the time to get to know the person and develop, if not a friendship, a cordial professional relationship. Relationships that are merely thinly disguised pitches for business are not genuine. People like working with people with whom they feel comfortable, and that takes a while to happen.

1. **Finding the relationships.** So, where will you find these people? Start with law school classmates with whom you had a good relationship in school. Focus first on those classmates who are practicing in the same geographical area as you, but don't limit yourself geographically. Particularly if you are with a specialty firm or you practice in a specialty area, maintaining relationships with classmates in distant cities can be fruitful as well. Regardless of geography, focus on classmates who are working for corporate firms serving business clients. You may have established good friendships in law school with classmates who have become public defenders, district attorneys, city attorneys, or attorneys for the state or federal government, and these contacts can be useful to have as you progress in the practice of law, but you will not likely develop much business from them.

You will want to focus on lawyers who represent business clients for two reasons. One, as those lawyers progress in their own firms, they might have an occasion to refer a client who needs a lawyer in your specialty area, or they might need to refer out a client because of a conflict of interest. The other reason is that lawyers who start their practice in corporate firms often go in-house eventually, and in such a role they would likely have the ability to hire outside counsel, that is, you. If you maintain a good relationship with them during the years they are with a law firm, you will be miles ahead of those attorneys who find them interesting only upon their becoming in-house counsel.

Also focus on college classmates with whom you are familiar, especially those who went on to work in business or became attorneys, accountants, or consultants. Don't limit yourself only to those who were good friends. If you played intercollegiate athletics, follow the career progress of your teammates. If you were a member of a fraternity or sorority, follow the careers of your fellow fraternity or sorority members. If you were in an organization composed of students from a particular race or ethnic background, follow the careers of your fellow organization members. If there is a local chapter of your college or university's alumni association, you should attend a meeting or two to determine whether you will meet other alumni there who might become prospective clients or referral sources down the road.

You should also attend young professionals' organizations in your city to scout potential contacts. Most larger nonprofit organizations, such as museums, community theaters, chambers of commerce, the United Way, the American Cancer Society, and similar organizations have young professionals chapters. Don't limit your network just to other attorneys, moreover. Think about the kinds of professionals who might need to refer a client to a lawyer like you. This would include doctors if you specialize in medical malpractice defense, human resources consultants if you specialize in employment law, or commercial insurance brokers if you specialize in insurance coverage disputes.

Finally, always be alert for an opportunity to meet another young professional or businessperson with whom you could build a business relationship. In this vein, wherever you go, *always carry your business cards!* You just never know. Shortly after I made partner in my firm, I decided to take a Saturday night off and go to a nightclub in downtown Los Angeles. I was single and noticed an attractive young woman across the way, so I asked her to dance. We danced for over an hour, and when we stopped to cool down, she said she was a CPA. I told her I needed to find a CPA to do my taxes now that I was a partner in a multistate law firm. She said her brother, also a CPA, had experience in preparing multistate taxes. I had my business cards with me, so I gave her one. It turned out our offices were literally next door, so we went to lunch one day, and afterward she introduced me to her brother the CPA—and to her other brother, who is an attorney and who also had just started out in the hotel business. Thirty years later, her one brother is still my CPA, and her other brother operates more than a dozen hotels in five states; his company has been my client almost since my meeting with his sister. So carry your business cards, people. Seriously.

2. Developing the relationships. There is no strict formula for developing a genuine relationship with a future client or referral source, other than that the relationship should be pursued only for the sake of the relationship, not with any apparent motive for soliciting business. The relationship can be initiated over lunch, coffee, or a cocktail after work. Catch up with what has been going on in the person's life. Learn about their work and what they find challenging about it. What are their ambitions? Inquire generally about their personal life: Married? Children? Parents? Extended family? Inquire about their interests and hobbies, in an attempt to find interests in common. Have they traveled recently for pleasure? Do they have any trips planned? Provide similar details regarding your work and after-work life.

When you return to your office, connect with the person on your LinkedIn account if you have not done so already. Also, make some notes regarding what was discussed during your meeting. Keep separate notes in a folder on your computer desktop about every such meeting you have and review your notes periodically. If the person told you about a particular challenge they were facing in their business or industry, record it, and should you happen onto an article on the issue, send it along. If the person said they would be going on a cruise over the summer or would be playing in a big amateur tennis tournament in the fall, follow up afterward with a brief email asking how it went. If you notice that they posted an accomplishment such as a promotion or a job change on LinkedIn, send a private note of congratulations. If you send paper or electronic holiday greetings, include them and add a personal note if possible. Schedule another in-person "catch-up" meeting, perhaps just over coffee or a cocktail, in about a year. You will want to show genuine interest in maintaining a professional relationship with the person without pushing too hard or it seeming contrived.

Should one of the persons with whom you have established a relationship reach out to you with a request or a question, respond promptly. Initially the request will not likely involve a referral or a piece of business. It will probably be something more mundane such as your child's experience at a prekindergarten they are considering, the name of the hotel in Paris where you said the service was awful, or the solicitation of a contribution for a nonprofit they are supporting. The prompt timing and helpfulness of your response will be appreciated and noted for future reference.

Not all of these relationships will result in new business for the firm. Regardless, you will still have a useful network of professionals whom you can call upon for information or assistance for yourself or for a client. It never hurts to be able to say, "I know a guy . . . ." Although your investment in these relationships might take years, some of them are very likely to result in new business coming to you. If you get started establishing these relationships in your first couple of years of law practice, they will ripen around the time when you will be expected to start bringing new business to the firm. You will not be like some of your colleagues who waited to focus on business development and now are struggling to establish relationships that might be able to deliver business in a hurry.

Bar and Community Involvement

Participating in bar and community organizations can expose you to potential clients and referral sources, but you have to be strategic about it. Participation in the Young Lawyers' Division of your state or local bar can help you meet junior lawyers in other fields of law with whom you might want to establish the kind of relationship described earlier. Participation in a bar section covering your practice area might be helpful toward your learning the subject area but not as useful in developing potential business later because the members of the section will consist of your competitors and your opposing counsel.

Participation in an Inns of Court chapter can be useful both for your professional development and for making contacts. Most Inns count judges and senior practitioners among their members, and these people can serve as valuable mentors to junior attorneys. Some cities have two or more Inns of Court; in that case, explore each of them before deciding which to join.

If you are in a jurisdiction that has mandatory continuing legal education (MCLE), your local bar association likely will sponsor seminars and webinars for MCLE credit. You will not likely have enough experience in your first few years to do such a presentation, but as you become more experienced in your subject area, these presentations can raise your profile in the local bar.

Specialty bar associations can provide a means of networking, mentoring, and relationship building among attorneys of the same race or ethnicity or other affinity group. Such organizations include the National Bar Association and local African-American bar associations (some of these are named after prominent African-American lawyers and judges, such as the John M. Langston Bar Association in Los Angeles and the Willkie D. Ferguson, Jr. Bar Association in Miami), Black Women Lawyers Associations, Hispanic Bar Associations, Korean American Bar Associations, Asian Pacific American Bar Associations, St. Thomas More Societies (for Catholic lawyers), and Lavender Bar Associations (for LGBTQ+ lawyers).

Involvement in community organizations can help you develop business if you serve on a key committee or can get onto the board of directors. Simply attending meetings of a chamber of commerce or fundraisers for local nonprofits will not likely move the needle for you in terms of business development. If you can score a key committee assignment or a board appointment, you will gain exposure to other board or committee members, most of whom will be local business leaders (and potential future clients or referral sources). It can take some time to gain an appointment to a nonprofit organization's board of directors, so you should evaluate how long it will take to gain such an appointment and the investment of time and money likely to be required, along with the likely benefit in terms of business development should you obtain a board appointment.

Becoming a Confident Public Speaker

You will have to become a confident public speaker in order to become a leading business developer for your firm. Part of developing business involves speaking before local, statewide, national, and international industry, trade, business, and bar organizations. You might not have to master this talent before becoming a partner, but if you do so sooner, it will only add further to your star quality.

Most audiences dread a presentation by a lawyer. So much legalese and dense explanation of boring topics. You can be different, though. You can develop and present content that is so different than the typical lawyer speech. In order to do so, you must first identify the practical point or points of your presentation that you want your audience to take away with them. Businesspeople don't want to hear a long exposition about the law. They want to know how the law will affect their business. Reduce the boring legalese to what it means practically for your audience. That will connect them with you initially.

Then you must be relatable. If you can add humor to the mix so that your audience might actually *enjoy* your presentation, you will stand out as a lawyer who can make law seem fun. Lawyers are not well trained in public speaking, however. Law school taught you only how to present at moot court, which is probably the worst training for public speaking one can imagine. Unless you already have a side gig at a comedy club, you will need to work on your public speaking skills.

The only way to become a confident public speaker is to speak in public. I admit that I was a painfully dull speaker as a young lawyer. If I could have bottled my audience's reactions to my presentations and sold them to insomniacs, I would not be writing this book now. I knew I had to get better at speaking, and I continued working at it. I offered to teach as an adjunct instructor at the local university, and they accepted my offer. For one night each week for 12 weeks, I had to take a group of midcareer professionals and keep them entertained for three hours after work when they were tired and hungry and just wanted to go home. But I learned how to connect with them and entertain them, and I ended up teaching for 16 years. The experience dramatically improved my speaking skills. In addition, several of my students became clients or came to work for my law firm.

Look for similar speaking opportunities if you need practice. Many universities have continuing education divisions that hire adjunct instructors to teach business-related courses to adult learners. Another option is Toastmasters. It is a nonprofit organization with hundreds of chapters in which members go to meetings simply to practice giving speeches to one another. I have known several people who went through the Toastmasters program, and it made them excellent public speakers.

When you are starting out as a public speaker, you should use a PowerPoint presentation with your talk. It will help you stay on track, and you will not have to memorize your speech verbatim, as you will have your slides to guide you from topic to topic. Do not put too much text on each slide, however. Do not quote long passages from statutes or cases on a PowerPoint slide. You will lose your audience. Rather, include only key words on each slide to communicate each topic. You will want your audience to hear what you have to say, not be busy trying to read dense text off your slides. Also, use stock photos to help communicate the concepts you are presenting. Your audience will connect better with your presentation if you include visual images related to your content. Commercial stock photo services offer hundreds of thousands of stock photos that you can use in your PowerPoint presentations for a nominal cost. As you become more confident as a speaker, you can try using some humorous images in your presentation as well. When you give a presentation with PowerPoint slides, either distribute paper copies of your slides to your audience or offer to send them an electronic copy of your presentation, and be sure to include your contact information on one of the slides (usually the last one).

Should you get an opportunity to speak publicly, at a local bar association MCLE program or a seminar or webinar[17] for your firm's clients, prepare thoroughly for it. Take the time to create a PowerPoint presentation that will engage your audience, and rehearse your presentation several times using the slides. When you give your presentation, do not read every slide, but refer to the slides as you speak. Know when the transitions from one topic to the next are supposed to occur so you will not be jumping all over the place disconnected from your slides. Avoid repeating yourself during your talk. Never say, "Like I said . . . ." If you said it once, that's enough. Practice the lead-in to your presentation. Make it short and compelling, not long and rambling. As you gain experience and confidence in public speaking, you will not have to spend as much time rehearsing for a presentation, but until you get there, invest the time necessary to ensure that your presentation will go smoothly. If it does, you will be that much more confident next time.

17. If you have a choice between presenting a webinar or a live seminar, always go with the live seminar. It is difficult to engage with an audience you cannot see on a webinar.

Writing and Publishing

Writing and publishing articles or book chapters on topics within your practice area can get you noticed by prospective clients. If you were involved in an interesting case or you have a unique perspective on a current issue in your area of the law, find a place to publish an article about it. The ABA and state and local bar associations are good places to start, as are organizations that focus on specific practice areas such as the National Association of Consumer Advocates or the Defense Research Institute. Law reviews focused on specific industries are worth exploring too, especially if they are accessible online.

When I was an associate, I was involved in a case in which airline pilots were calling in sick in higher than usual numbers during labor contract negotiations with my firm's airline client. Special labor laws cover airline and railroad employees, and those laws prohibit employee strikes unless and until a lengthy process to try to reach an agreement has been exhausted. Sometimes airline employees will try to put pressure on the airline earlier during negotiations by calling in sick in large numbers. An airline can get a court to enjoin such a job action if it can prove that it was concerted and intentional, but that can be difficult. We retained a statistical expert who developed a statistical model to show that the likelihood of such a large number of pilot call-outs being coincidental was infinitesimally small, and his analysis convinced a federal judge to issue an injunction. I then wrote an article with the statistician for an industry publication that explained our approach. About a year later, a leading U.S. airline contacted me when it was facing a potential for the same kind of job action. If you have worked on a case whose outcome benefited a particular industry, write about it.[18] Others in the industry might be interested, and they might become clients as a result.

18. You will need your client's approval to write about a specific case involving them, and clients often are reluctant to give such approval. You could still write about the theory or approach you pursued in general terms, however, which is what I did in the article I wrote with the statistician.

Entertaining Clients

Fortunately, the three-martini lunch is now a relic of history. Client meals and entertainment are still an important tool of business development, though. You should learn whether your firm has any formal rules or guidelines involving client meals and entertainment. If your firm does not have formal rules, the use of good judgment is the best standard to apply. If you are ever unsure, ask for guidance.

Some clients have strict rules regarding what their employees may accept in terms of meals and entertainment from vendors, including lawyers. Many public sector employees are barred from receiving free meals from their lawyers. If you go to lunch with a friend from the city attorney's office, expect that you both will probably have to pay your own way, and choose the restaurant accordingly. Many publicly traded (and even some privately held) corporations have rules on what their employees may accept. Lunch is usually OK, but a lavish dinner, World Series tickets, or an expensive bottle of wine is not. These restrictions are typically found in the corporation's code of ethics applicable to all employees, and they are designed to prevent bribery or even the appearance of undue influence on corporate decision-making.

If you are meeting with a client and you and the client go to lunch afterward, always offer to pick up the tab. If the client insists, allow them to pay, but in most cases the client will allow you to beat them to it. Submit the receipt to your firm for reimbursement, and you should receive payment. Likewise, if you are meeting with clients in the firm's offices, offer to have lunch delivered and either pay for it or have it charged to the firm. The firm will reimburse you for lunches with genuine *prospective* clients too, but don't abuse the privilege by submitting a receipt for lunch with a relative or old friend who is not likely ever to become a client of the firm.

Sometimes the most effective client entertainment is where you are able to share with a client an activity you both enjoy, such as a round of golf, a wine tasting event, a sporting event, or something similar. These experiences should be reserved for client representatives with whom you have established a strong working relationship. Inviting the client representative for such an outing should seem natural, not contrived. If you are a decent golfer and your client drops the hint that he would like to play a course in your city sometime, an invitation to play at that course would be the natural follow-up. If you learn that a client representative will be attending your firm's client conference event and you know she is a fan of good wines, you might consider organizing a small trip for a few clients and a few attorneys from your firm to a nearby winery and inviting her. If you know your client is a big Heat fan and you know he will be visiting Los Angeles when the Heat are playing the Lakers, invite him to the game as your guest. These overtures can cement a relationship with an important client representative. If you did not originate the client yourself, however, be sure the client's relationship partner is on board with what you are planning.

Once considered routine, holiday gifts for clients can be awkward today. Many clients do not allow their employees to accept them, or they place a low limit on the value of a gift that may be accepted, or they require that gifts of food or wine be shared with all employees in the office or department. Giving a client representative a holiday gift can make the person feel uncomfortable, moreover. A client receiving such a gift might believe that something is expected in return. Other client representatives might have come to expect gifts from outside counsel around the holidays if they had been provided consistently before. If you are unsure whether a client gift might be expected or allowed, ask the partner in charge of the client relationship. The question is likely to have come up before. Sometimes law firms try to avoid this problem by making a contribution to a nonprofit organization and then noting the contribution in an electronic or paper holiday card that attorneys can send to clients. If your firm does so, take advantage of the opportunity to reach out to your client contacts and prospective clients with one of the firm's greetings.

Finally, you might encounter the situation where the client representative with whom you work asks you for a gift, such as tickets for a theater production or a sporting event. In this situation, he is not suggesting you invite him, he is asking for you to give him the tickets for his own use. If this occurs, you must notify the relationship partner for the client. A partner will have to approve such an expenditure, and the relationship partner will have to make the judgment whether such a gift may even be provided under the client's code of ethics. You should not make that determination on your own.

11

After Hours

Law firm life is not *all* work. You will still have time for personal pursuits and for a social life. What you do in your free time can have an impact on your career trajectory, though. You are similar to a professional athlete in that you must stay focused on your game. You cannot afford to let outside distractions interfere with your focus. Moreover, as an attorney in a leading law firm, you will never be 100 percent "off duty." You will be held to a higher standard of conduct than the general public even when you are not working.

Socializing with Your Colleagues

Your firm will likely put on various mixers and events to help you and other new associates get to know other attorneys in the firm. You should attend those events. You will not connect with everyone you meet, but you will connect with a few. Follow up with them with an invitation to coffee or lunch. The sooner you start building your network, the better.

Sometimes, a group of associates will go out socializing after work. Participate in those outings, but do not mistake them for get-togethers with good friends. Any inappropriate conduct or conversation on your part might be used against you later. Be mindful of your alcohol intake. If you begin to lose your inhibitions after your second drink, don't have more than one.[19] Absolutely do not use any illegal substances even if others are using them. Do not flirt with other associates. Be circumspect regarding what you talk about. Stick to topics that will help you find things in common with the others, such as where you grew up, schools you attended, unique travel experiences you have had, your hobbies and interests, and your favorite sports teams. Avoid discussing politics and uncomfortable personal topics such as illnesses, divorce, or relationship issues. Don't discuss your younger, wilder days, even if you are asked. Talking about how you used to get drunk in college or smoked weed or did mushrooms will not make you more relatable. Worse, some of your colleagues in attendance will file away the information in case it should become useful later. You never know who will be a rival for a job, be competing for a client relationship, or even be a client five or ten years down the road.

When out with colleagues, always bring your best. Be courteous to bartenders and servers, tip well, and avoid conflicts with other patrons. You may think you are in a restaurant or bar, but you are really in an extension of your work environment. Behave accordingly. Also, if you notice that a colleague has been overserved, be sure he or she has a safe way home afterward, even if you have to pay for an Uber or a taxi ride. You will help prevent a potential tragedy, and your kindness and concern will be returned.

Dating Your Colleagues

After spending long days working alongside other associates at the firm, you might well become attracted to one or more of them and even consider dating them. Is this a good idea?

Generally, no. After you both spend all day in the same pressure cooker, what are you going to talk about after hours? There is only so much office gossip to discuss. If you are thinking of becoming involved with another associate, keep in mind that lawyers tend

19. A ginger ale on ice with a lime will allow you to remain sober while making others think you are enjoying an alcoholic cocktail.

to be competitive, and they are trained to win in adversarial settings. What will happen if your partner scores the big case assignment you were hoping to get?

Granted, I know a few happy couples who met as lawyers at the same firm, fell in love, and have lived in married bliss (more or less) ever since. Sometimes it takes a lawyer to really understand another lawyer. I have watched employees of numerous clients similarly meet at work and marry and remain together. Having the same profession could make it easier to relate to one another and stay together.

If you feel this forever potential with another associate at your firm, then see where it might go, but don't date another associate in your firm simply because it's easier than finding people to date outside of work. In the latter situation your dating relationship will likely end eventually, and then you will have an awkwardness with your colleague that could make it uncomfortable for you at the office. You do not need such distraction and potential disruption of your forward progress at the firm.

What about dating support staff at your firm? Don't go there. It is likely to become a source of gossip, and you do not want that kind of attention. Also, if you decide to end the relationship, don't be surprised if the staff person complains to human resources that he or she felt sexually harassed. It happens more than you might imagine. Maybe you will be cleared, but being the subject of a sexual harassment investigation is not the best career move for an associate in a law firm. If you and the staff member simply cannot resist one another, suggest that the staff member find a position in another law firm.

The same goes for dating a partner. The firm probably has a policy against it, and if the relationship is discovered, it will be the source of drama and gossip. Your peers may believe you benefit from favoritism, whether or not it actually exists. All of this could well diminish your credibility in the firm and damage your relationships with your colleagues. Also, if (when) the relationship ends, it could be difficult for you and the partner to work together again. You might lose a valuable mentor.

What about asking out that gorgeous opposing counsel in one of your cases? That's unethical in most jurisdictions, at least while the case is still ongoing. You must cool your passion until the case has been settled (with settlement funds paid and case dismissed with prejudice) or finally resolved in court (with all appeal periods expired).

What about dating an attorney in another firm? That is less problematic, so long as your two firms are not opposing one another in a current case. If they are but neither of you is working on the case, it might still be OK, but you should check with your supervising partner or your office managing partner. Your firm might have to erect an ethical "screen" to ensure you do not become involved in the case.

Finally, what about dating a client? Ethical rules in many states prohibit intimate relationships between attorneys and clients. Where the client is an organization, the prohibition applies to the client representative or decision-maker on the matter. Even if your intended paramour is not the client representative in your case but another employee of the client, you should still tread carefully, especially if you did not originate the client. There is no better way to alienate a partner in your law firm than to have that partner's client fire your firm because of relationship drama involving you and one of the client's employees.

If all of this sounds complicated, it is. Because lawyers are fiduciaries, dating lawyers outside your firm or employees of clients can violate various ethical rules. Also, today's sexual harassment laws make dating others at your firm much more perilous than it was a generation ago. Because your goal as an associate is to advance in the firm and internal gossip, drama, and even potential HR investigations will likely hold you back, dating inside your firm is not a good idea. If you are still single, therefore, finding a significant other who is not a lawyer and who does not work for a firm client might be your best bet. Putting work aside for a time to go meet some new people will be healthy for you anyway.

Your Outside Activities

The practice of law might seem all-consuming in your first few years, but you should try to maintain hobbies and interests outside of work. Playing sports, watching sports, going to a gym, participating in the arts and culture, becoming involved with community organizations or nonprofits, or attending religious services all can help provide some balance in your life and help you manage the stress of practicing law. What you do on your own time is your business, but you should use care that your off-duty pursuits do not come back to your firm and reflect poorly on you.

You must avoid conduct that is criminal or irresponsible or that shows bad judgment on your part. Examples include driving under the influence, leaving the scene of an accident, acts of road rage, domestic violence, public intoxication, involvement in physical altercations, and loud profane rants against store clerks or other service workers. Remember that video surveillance cameras are everywhere today, and whatever you say or do is likely to be recorded. Because attorneys are often held to a higher standard, your misconduct is going to be more newsworthy than that of an electrician or a warehouse worker. You don't want to be featured on a viral internet post or the evening news as an example of a lawyer behaving badly.

Use care also in your financial affairs. Don't overextend yourself financially such that you cannot meet your obligations and might have to file for personal bankruptcy. You do not need a fancy apartment, an expensive car, or designer clothing when you are just starting your career. All of that can come later, but you must earn it. Meanwhile, live within your means and remember that credit card companies are not your friends. You'll need a credit card and a backup for business travel and entertainment, but you should avoid having more than two credit cards if you can. If you have money to invest, invest carefully. Stay away from shady schemes that sound too good to be true or that might be in tomorrow's headlines. If you are going to invest in the stock market, be mindful of the laws against insider trading. You expose yourself to potential liability under those laws by trading in the stock of your firm's clients. Don't do it.

Finally, choose your friends—and, if you are single, your dating partners—carefully. Avoid people who drink heavily, use mind-altering substances, party all night, or engage in dangerous or reckless activities. You cannot be a part of that lifestyle and still be the high-functioning lawyer that you need to be if you are going to be a star associate. Find romantic partners who will bring calm and happiness into your life, not chaos and turmoil. After working so hard through college and law school and now at the firm, you might be tempted to want to "live a little" and pick a partner who is a sexy free spirit and the complete opposite of you. For a while the experience will be exhilarating, but then it will crash when it becomes apparent that you both are so incompatible. You can't just pick up and fly to Ibiza with them next week because you have to *work*, and when you went out with their friends, you were left with a bar tab that exceeded your monthly salary. If you are lucky, when the relationship ends you will be left only heartbroken and emotionally exhausted. If you are unlucky, you might also be left broke and with an arrest record, too.

Social Media

You must use care regarding what you post on social media. Even if you do not identify your affiliation with your law firm or even indicate that you are an attorney, what you post online can still come back to you at your firm. Avoid posting content about your firm or your work on most social media. The only exception is LinkedIn, where you can mention your firm affiliation as well as professional achievements and recognitions you have received, but you should avoid discussing the specifics of your work for identifiable clients. Many clients do not want their law firms publishing their litigation results, for example, even where the result is a victory.

You should never post information online that is critical of your clients or your law firm. Your clients may not be perfect, but dissing them online will get you fired. Also avoid posting on websites that specialize in embarrassing law firms or that serve as vehicles for unhappy associates to complain about their firms. This includes "anonymous" posts. You might think you are anonymous, but, depending on the content, it could nonetheless be obvious who posted it.

You must also avoid posting content online that takes extreme social or political positions or that could be interpreted as racist, sexist, hateful, or biased against any person or group based on their nationality, ancestry, religion, immigration status, sexual orientation, gender identity, or the like. Similarly, you should avoid posting content that advocates for the overthrow or disruption of the U.S. government or that expresses advocacy or sympathy for terrorists or those committing violent criminal acts. Yes, I know there is a First Amendment and you have the right to say just about anything you want. But as you will recall from your Con Law course, the First Amendment prevents only the *government* from interfering with your speech, not private individuals or organizations. A law firm or its clients are free to decide not to associate with someone who advocates publicly for extreme positions. Just ask the law student whose job offer from a top-tier law firm was withdrawn after they published a letter online condemning Israel for the attack by Hamas terrorists on that country in October 2023. Cancel culture exists on both ends of the political spectrum. Most law firms allow their attorneys leeway to participate in debate about the issues of the day, but if you go too far in either direction, there is the potential that those on the other side of the issue might confront your firm or its clients with what you said in an attempt to cancel you. Even if that does not occur, a client could read what you posted and react negatively to it. While it might make you feel good to speak your piece online, you could be inflicting significant harm on your career. Consider keeping your voice out of the debate.

You also should be cautious about who you "friend" or allow to "follow" you on social media sites such as Facebook and Instagram. Typically, you should not connect with other attorneys or staff at your law firm or your clients at the firm unless you have become good friends outside of work. Why? If you post photos and stories about your awesome vacations, your new car, or the trendy restaurants you frequent, it might cause jealousy or resentment on the part of your fellow associates, support staff at your firm, and even some clients. As you progress up the career ladder and your compensation increases, you will be able to afford things that others around you will not. Likewise with respect to posting your engagement or wedding photos or photos of your children. Not everyone has found their life's love or has been able to start a family. By sharing your life successes on social media with those with whom you work, you potentially put distance between yourself and other people who are not so fortunate but whom you will need to succeed in your career. Where social media is concerned, it's best to keep the boundary intact between your business life and your personal life.

Talking Out of School

Over the course of your career, you likely will work on some matters of great consequence. That work might even come while you are still an associate. If it does, you might be tempted to brag to your family and friends about the importance of the work you are doing. You must be careful what you say to others about your work, however. You could cause serious harm to a client by leaking information about sensitive matters your firm is handling for that client.

Whether you are talking with a dinner date, a significant other, or an old friend, you must be very circumspect about your work. You cannot afford to be the source of a breach of confidentiality that exposes a client's plans for acquisition of a competitor, a massive employee layoff, or the introduction of a game-changing new technology. Even if you do not reveal the name of the client, it might still be possible for others to identify the client through the information you reveal.

The same goes for your family. They will be very proud of you and want to hear all about your work as a big firm lawyer, especially at family gatherings over the holidays. You cannot trust even your family to keep confidential any information you reveal, however. Your dad might talk with his golfing buddies about you. Your mom might brag to her coworkers about the impressive work you are doing. Your sister's date for Thanksgiving might buy or sell stock on the information you reveal (and that's illegal). You must not provide details, therefore, about the work you do or the identity of your clients. Never reveal sensitive information about a client's current affairs or future plans or the complex legal problems you are working on, no matter how exciting the work or how instrumental your role. If you must, pretend that you work for the CIA or at Area 51. You must maintain the same secrecy about your work as a lawyer.

Likewise, use care in what you say to colleagues or staff about your clients and your work when you are in elevators, in your building lobby, and even in your own office suite reception area. You never know who might be listening. On most days in a large law firm, there are opposing counsel as well as counsel for other businesses present for various depositions and meetings. Resist the urge, therefore, to say to colleagues while waiting for an elevator, "You won't believe the stupid thing our client did!" Even if you are not overheard by anyone who could use the information to your client's detriment, it makes you appear unprofessional.

Practicing Law for Friends and Family

Once the world learns you are a lawyer, you will have an endless stream of family members, friends, significant others, occasional acquaintances, and perfect strangers seeking free legal services from you. Your brother bought a car that turned out to be a "lemon." The woman you are dating wants to sue her boss for sexual harassment. Your parents' insurance claim from the hurricane still has not been paid. The barista at your favorite coffee house is being "unfairly" evicted from her apartment. Your college roommate has a startup and wants you to review the lease for his new company space.

You will be quite tempted to help these people with their legal problems. Giving back is the least you can do, correct? Especially where family is involved, right? What harm would there be if I just wrote a strong letter on behalf of my family member or friend? When performing free legal services for friends and family, though, remember the rule that applies to so much of life: No good deed goes unpunished. Doing side legal work when you are in a law firm is a bad idea. Doing side legal work when you are a junior associate in a law firm still learning about the practice of law is an even worse idea. To start, your firm probably has a policy against it. Many firms prohibit their lawyers from performing legal services except through the law firm, with an exception only for approved pro bono activities. Even if your firm has no such policy, it's still a bad idea.

First, you run the risk of conflicts of interest. Most larger law firms represent a wide variety of businesses and organizations. Your firm might already represent the manufacturer of your brother's car, your parents' insurer, or the owner of the apartments where the barista lives. If that is the case, you will have an ethical conflict because, as you learned when you studied for the MPRE, a conflict on the part of one lawyer in a firm extends to all of the lawyers in the firm. You will also have a practical conflict with the partner in your firm who has the client relationship. He or she will likely receive a call from an irritated client who just learned that an associate from your firm is threatening to sue them. You might say, "Well, I would never use the firm's name in my pursuit of justice for my family or friends." Perhaps not, but it's not that simple. Most state bars now list all attorneys admitted in the state on the bar's website, and the listings typically include the attorney's firm affiliation. It will not be difficult for the recipient of your demand letter to find out where you work.

Second, even if your firm does not currently represent the target of your demand for justice, it might have an opportunity to do so in the future. The partners in your firm are always in the hunt for new client relationships, and each such new relationship is put through a conflict check as part of the new client intake process. How will you respond when you learn that a partner in your firm just landed the insurance company to which you wrote a demand letter on behalf of your parents? If your firm publishes new clients to all attorneys, you would have an obligation to notify the firm about your representation of your parents, and the partner likely will lose the new client relationship. Even if you were to offer to get new counsel for Mom and Dad immediately to avoid the conflict, the insurance company might still decide to seek counsel elsewhere. It would be even worse if you did not know of the new client relationship at the outset but the conflict was to be discovered later, after your firm already was performing work for the new client. Your firm might have to withdraw from the representation and refund any fees paid by the client in the best-case scenario. Your firm might be sued for malpractice in the worst case. Either way, your employment with the firm would not likely last long enough for you to learn firsthand how the mess was resolved.

Third, even if there are no conflicts now or in the future, ask yourself if you really are doing your friend or family member a service by attempting to represent them in an area of law in which you have little or no knowledge and experience. Moreover, when the insurance company receives the demand letter from you on behalf of your parents who just happen to have the same last name as you, are they going to take it seriously? My clients over the years have received numerous demand letters written by lawyers who are obviously friends or relatives of their "client." These letters are not taken as seriously as a letter from an arm's-length attorney. That's not to say the matter about which you write will be ignored, but the recipient will probably conclude, and accurately so, that you will not actually file a lawsuit if the matter is not resolved to your complete satisfaction.

Fourth, what if you make a mistake? What if you miss a statute of limitations, fail to exhaust administrative or internal remedies, or fail to advise your client to attempt to mitigate her damages? What if your lawsuit fails to seek all available types of monetary relief and you settle the case for less than you could have received if it had been properly pled? What if you failed to recognize the significance of a clause in your friend's lease that enabled the landlord to terminate the lease and evict your friend's startup for a nonconforming use without any opportunity to cure? Your once-grateful client might decide to sue you for malpractice. If they sue your firm too, that would be bad news. If they sue only you, that would be worse news because your firm's malpractice insurance would not likely cover you while you were freelancing.

The bottom line here is that you should not be doing legal work on the side for friends or family. You are much better off assisting your relatives, friends, and acquaintances in finding the right attorney, who is experienced in the area of law governing their issue, to represent them. Most attorneys who represent consumers or employees do so on a contingent fee basis, so there is no cost to the client up front. Such an attorney would be a much better option than you in most situations.

What if a nonprofit organization where you volunteer, the community theater you frequent, or the daycare center operated by your place of worship asks you to provide legal advice or services on a pro bono basis? Check with your law firm. Your firm might well accept the organization as a pro bono client and approve your doing the work, provided it is in an area of the law with which you are familiar and you are adequately supervised by a partner. Most firms are pleased to provide pro bono services for worthy nonprofits and community organizations so long as there are no conflicts of interest and they can be sure that the services will be performed in a competent manner. If your firm allows you to perform services on a pro bono basis, be sure you are sufficiently knowledgeable and experienced to perform the work involved. If you are not, ask your firm for assistance from a lawyer with the appropriate experience and expertise.

Taking Time Off

You will need to take time off from the firm to relax and recharge. Even though you will be very busy, you must find time on your calendar to take some vacation. Take a trip somewhere so you can truly get away. When you arrive, it will probably take you a couple of days to get into relaxation mode; it's not unlike stepping off one of those moving sidewalks at the airport. Take enough time so you will have time to relax. Then try to get out of work mode as much as possible. Take along some books (*not* about law) you've been wanting to read. Get out into nature and get some exercise. Catch up on sleep. Enjoy the local cuisine. Talk like a normal person, not like a lawyer.

Once you lock in the dates and make travel plans, resist the urge to cancel or change them for work, especially if family or your significant other will be traveling with you. Unfortunately, sometimes circumstances will require that you change your plans where an important firm client is involved and your role in the matter is integral, but those situations are rare. When in doubt, have a candid conversation with the supervising partner. If you must change your plans, you will have demonstrated your commitment to the firm and its client by doing so.

Assuming you will be able to escape without any last-minute diversions, keep in mind that you cannot disappear from the grid completely. Partners and senior associates typically have to take their laptop computers with them on vacation and check in every day. As a junior associate, you will not yet likely have the level of responsibility for cases and matters requiring that, but it might be necessary for a partner or other lawyer to contact you while you are away to check on the status of a matter you are handling. Keep your cell phone with you on vacation, therefore, and be alert for work-related calls and texts. Leave your itinerary with your assistant and indicate if there will be any days when you will not have cell service. On those days provide an alternate number where you can be reached if necessary. Firm personnel will not call you while you are on vacation unless it is absolutely necessary, but sometimes it will be necessary, especially as your level of responsibility increases. Associates occasionally chafe at this advice, but you must remember that you are a professional handling important matters for clients and sometimes things come up that cannot wait for your return. Your graciously taking the call or answering the text message while on vacation will only confirm your star potential.

12

Maybe You're in the Wrong Firm

If you have read the first 11 chapters of this book thinking, "The firm where I work is nothing like what he describes," you might be in the wrong law firm. There are reasons to consider switching firms. We will discuss those reasons here. There are reasons why you should not switch firms, too, chief of which is to be paid more money. If you are unsure whether you are in the right firm, now is the time to decide. If you must move firms, the longer you wait, the more it will affect the forward progress of your career.

The Grass Isn't Greener

Most associates consider switching firms at some point. Sometimes it's because they are in a truly bad place, where the firm is not what it appeared to be during the recruiting process. Sometimes it's because of a fit of pique. The firm won't let you work remotely, one of the partners you work with is difficult, or your mentor told you to get a haircut or dress more professionally when you come to the office, so you decide to shop for a firm that allows its associates more flexibility, has nicer partners, or does not interfere with your self-expression. Sometimes associates look at other options not because anything is particularly wrong at their current firm, but because they perceive another firm as simply a "better" firm however they define it—larger, smaller, more prestigious, a lower billable hours expectation.

Changing law firms is like changing relationship partners. You might find someone new who does not have that annoying habit your former partner had that irritated you so much, but your new partner has a whole new range of issues that you wish you had known about before you made the switch. Just as no relationship is perfect, no law firm is perfect. Every firm has its flaws. What you must decide is whether, when all of the firm's positives and negatives are taken into account, the firm where you are is the best fit for *you*.

Keep in mind, too, that if you switch law firms, in many respects you will be starting over. You will bring your legal skills and experience that you have developed, but you will have to reestablish an internal network and your reputation in your new firm. You will have to learn the work styles of a new group of partners, and you will have to find new mentors. Sometimes such a new start is necessary where your old firm is simply not a good fit, but too much moving about various law firms as an associate will have you spending your time becoming adjusted to new firms and new people instead of further developing your skills and experience as a lawyer.

Work is work. Law firm work is stressful. That's why you are paid more than marketing professionals, teachers, journalists, and interior designers. Not only is the work challenging, but also in a law firm you are not just working a job. You are a member of a profession where you often must go above and beyond to protect the interests of your clients. Like a doctor who cannot leave her critically ill patient simply because it's 5 p.m., you have to be available to work when the firm needs you, which sometimes means weekends and holidays. You must work around high-achieving, competitive people who are used to winning, and the personalities of such people are not always laid back and chill. Moreover, the firm is a business. The partners are its owners, and they want to make money. This requires that all of the firm's lawyers be highly productive and accountable, including you.

If you are considering changing firms, give careful thought to the reasons why. Are you making a mature and informed decision about your career, or are you reacting to a disappointment or slight that is not really all that important in the bigger picture? Make a list of the positive attributes of your current firm and its negatives in two columns. Be honest and objective. Which list is longer? Even if the list of negative attributes is shorter but you feel that some of them are things you cannot live with, be realistic about whether you will likely find those negative attributes in other firms. If you decide to interview with other firms, be sure to look for those negative attributes, as you might well find them to be present in those firms too.

It might be that your discontent with your firm is not so much reflective of the firm as it is reflective of law firm practice. Maybe you are simply not happy working in a law firm. Perhaps you would be happier working in-house, in government service, or in your own small firm. All of these options carry downsides as well as upsides, so if you are contemplating a career change of this type, be sure it's with eyes wide open.

Attorneys who go in-house often expect to gain more work-life balance and work fewer hours. Sometimes that happens, sometimes not. In-house legal departments are rarely overstaffed. You will likely have a limited budget for outside counsel, and you will not have 15 or more lawyers down the hall practicing in the same area of law as you whom you can consult regarding difficult issues. You will have multiple business unit clients internally, all with time-sensitive needs. Your compensation as an in-house lawyer is likely to be lower than what the firm pays you, too. If you receive stock or stock options as an in-house attorney, though, you will have the potential to build long-term wealth if the company thrives.

Attorneys who enter government service are sometimes able to represent the public interest in important areas of the law, such as civil rights or environmental law. They might also carry out criminal prosecutions (as deputy district attorneys or assistant U.S. attorneys) or be involved in national security matters (as an attorney for the Department of State, the Department of Defense, or related agencies). Not all government lawyer jobs are so exciting or fulfilling, however. Some can be quite mundane, and as a government attorney, your opportunities for advancement and increased compensation might be limited.

Hanging your own shingle as a solo practitioner seems appealing to many lawyers, but if you go that route, the financial risk is wholly your own. You must rent office space; hire an assistant; acquire office furnishings and equipment; obtain software for filing, calendaring, timekeeping, and billing; and buy malpractice insurance before you can open for business. If you do not bring clients to your solo practice who are willing to pay you on an hourly basis, you will be working primarily on contingent fee matters. You will have to find and screen clients and begin pursuing their claims. Several months likely will go by before you generate any revenue. You must have the financial resources to make it through this initial period. Once up and running, some contingent fee lawyers become very successful by finding clients with high-value claims and taking a percentage. Not all such lawyers find such a practice to be lucrative, however.

Before you leave your law firm to embark on a different kind of legal career, therefore, do your research. Talk with attorneys who work in the role you are considering, so you are clear on the pros and cons of their type of law practice. Be sure that the move is the right one for you, because it can be difficult to reenter law firm practice after you have left it for any length of time, if you find you really prefer to work in a law firm after all.

Never Leave the Right Firm for More Money

Associates are often tempted to switch firms for more money. This is almost never a good idea. Most associates today are bombarded by calls from legal recruiters. The calls can seem flattering initially, perhaps leading you to think that maybe you *are* worth more than you are currently being paid and that you are leaving money on the table by staying at your current firm.

First, don't be flattered. That same recruiter likely pitched the same message to several other associates at your law firm. There is nothing special about you, a junior associate, in the eyes of the recruiter or in the eyes of the law firm he is recruiting for. It's not like you have had time yet to win a few jury trials, argue a groundbreaking case in the court of appeals, or land a high-profile new client for your firm. At this early point in your career, you are still fungible. The recruiter is not looking for *you*, specifically; he is looking for corporate associates, litigation associates, or associates who speak Spanish or who have a science background.

Second, don't fall for the sales pitch. The recruiter will tell you that the (usually unnamed) firm he represents is a "leading firm in the region" offering a "phenomenal opportunity" to talented associates like yourself. If the firm is such a leader, though, and the opportunity is so phenomenal, why is he trying to pitch it door to door to associates in your firm and others like an encyclopedia salesperson from another era? And why is the *primary* reason you should join this firm that they will pay you more money than your current firm pays you?

Third, find out what you are going to have to do for the big pay raise if you join the firm the recruiter is pitching. Law firms do not give money to associates for free. Ask the recruiter how many hours you will be expected to bill at this new firm should you join it. Ask the recruiter what kind of work you will be doing at the new firm. Will you have your own cases? Will you get to go to trial as an associate? Will you have direct client contact in each of your cases? If you will be a corporate associate, will you be a part of M&A deal teams? And while we are on the topic of opportunity, ask the recruiter if you will be eligible to make partner at this new firm sooner than at your current firm. If the recruiter cannot give you clear answers to these questions, ask him to find out and get back to you.

By now you probably get the point. Law firms that truly offer associates extraordinary opportunities for professional development and advancement don't need to go door to door at other law firms attempting to lure associates with promises of more money. If you picked your current firm carefully as I recommended in Chapter 1, you might be able to get more money if you leave your firm for another firm, but you will probably get less of something else that is important to you, such as free time, interesting work, hands-on experience, training and mentoring, client contact, or partnership potential.

If you think you are with the right firm for you, therefore, don't leave the firm for more money somewhere else. You knew your current firm's pay structure when you joined it, and you should have determined at that time that what you would be paid would square with your budget. If you are now strapped financially, ask yourself why. Did you buy a home too soon, or are you living in an apartment you cannot afford? Did you buy an expensive car? Do you take expensive trips or frequent expensive restaurants? Try your best to reduce your costs before you leave your firm for more money. Accept some short-term pain for long-term gain. Skip the trip to Italy this year, start cooking more at home, and if your expensive home or apartment has extra room, consider getting a roommate.

I know, sometimes life surprises you. You became a parent sooner than you expected, or one of your parents has fallen ill and needs in-home care. Your spouse lost his job, and new jobs in his field are scarce right now. Many of you still have student debt to retire as well. You might come to believe that your only option is to find a firm that will pay you more. Before you go down that road and leave a firm that's otherwise a good fit for you, though, be sure that doing so is your only option for dealing with your current financial predicament.

Finally, if you must leave for more money, do so in an honorable fashion. Give your current firm plenty of notice, help to transition your cases and projects, and don't speak negatively about the firm to others or online. Shake hands with your office's managing partner when you leave and thank him or her for the great experience and opportunities the firm provided you. If you were a valued associate and you left on good terms, you will be welcomed back should you wish to return when your financial situation stabilizes. I always love it when an associate leaves our firm for more money and then comes back to us (and our pay scale) in a year or two. It is proof we are doing something right.

When It's Really Not the Right Firm for You

It's not just the money, you're thinking. There are other things about this firm that make it a bad fit for me. Maybe the firm seems unstable. A significant amount of turnover among firm partners is not a good sign, especially among partners in leadership roles in the firm. Layoffs of attorneys or staff are a bad sign too. Perhaps there is no realistic path for you to become a partner at the firm. This can be the case with very large firms and with much smaller but successful firms where the founders of the firm are still running it and little attention is paid to developing future owners and leaders of the firm. Maybe there is no emphasis on training or mentoring of associates, and all anyone cares about is whether you are billing hours. Maybe you are a diverse attorney, and the firm devotes little or no effort toward the recruitment and success of diverse associates. Perhaps the firm has a toxic working environment where partners are allowed to bully and demean associates and staff. If you really cannot see a future career path for yourself at the firm, then you must look at other options. Read Chapter 1 of this book again and then take your time to find a firm that is a better fit for you.

As you search for a new firm, stay focused not just on finding another law firm job but on finding a firm where you can become a star. Find a firm that will actively assist you in developing your career, a firm that will provide you with opportunities to grow and succeed professionally. Find a firm where you have a real chance of making partner if you work hard and produce excellent results. Follow your instinct as you speak with recruiters and as you visit potential new firms and talk with their attorneys. Does it feel right or not? If not, keep looking. Better to continue searching now than having to start a new search a year from now.

Now that you "get it," you know what to look for. If you don't have it, go find it.

Index